FOUNDATIONS

of Faith and Family

A Biblical Guide to
Generational Wealth

FOUNDATIONS
of Faith and Family

A Biblical Guide to
Generational Wealth

Dr. Gordon Lesley Rolls

Foundations of Faith and Family
A Biblical Guide to Generational Wealth

ISBN: 978-81-19524-15-0

First published in India in 2024 by Exceller Books,
An imprint of GE Group

Address: G1, Dream Apartment, Degree College Road, Belgharia, Kolkata, 700056, India
www.excellerbooks.com

Acknowledgements

I would like to express my deepest gratitude and appreciation to the following individuals and groups who have supported me throughout the creation of this book.

- First and foremost, I thank my Heavenly Father, God Almighty, for His guidance, inspiration, and the opportunity to empower the body of Christ through this work.
- To my wife and children, thank you for your unwavering support, understanding, and prayers as I dedicated countless hours to working on this project.
- I want to give special thanks to my brothers, Dr. Leon Rolls, Derrick Rolls, and Martin Rolls, for their constant encouragement and motivation.
- I am grateful to my prayer partners, friends, and the entire IEMA and DOCSA family for being a source of great support and encouragement.
- A heartfelt thank you to my mentor, Dr. Abu Bako, for his prayers, guidance, and inspiration that have fueled my journey.
- To my spiritual parents in the Ministry, Dr. Helena Strachan and Pastor Stanley Strachan, I am forever thankful for your wisdom and support.

- To my dear friend and confidant, Mabrouk Issa Mabrouk, thank you for always being there for me. Your friendship means the world to me.
- I thank the Osman family for their love and unwavering support throughout this endeavour.
- Finally, I dedicate this book to the loving memory of my late mother and brother. Your love and presence continue to inspire me every day.

Thank you to everyone who has contributed to this journey. Your contributions have made this book possible.

Foreword

"When you acquire an appliance and don't exploit the capacities and possibilities offered by that appliance as outlined in the user manual, it is highly probable that you will either misuse or under-utilize it, leading to limited utility, short-lived use or undue destruction."

Marriage and the Family are God's idea; the cattle on a thousand hills belong to Him; and approaching issues related to the family and wealth using another lens apart from God's own as clearly reflected by His word - the Bible will often result in stunted outputs or the abysmal results we observe in many families today.

No one would have said this better than Rev. Dr. Gordon Rolls in this beautiful volume in your hands, which is the first of a series of books he will enrich your library with.

Dr Rolls and I have both fraternized in kingdom affairs as well as synergized in the domains of leadership and relationships/family life for a while now. He has been a tremendous blessing to couples during our annual "Couples Forum", when he and his wife have been resource persons.

In the book "FOUNDATIONS OF FAITH AND FAMILY: A Biblical Guide to Generational Wealth", Rev Dr Rolls redirects our focus to God's idea about this sacred institution of the family, which is the nucleus of society. He beautifully combines a powerful spiritual and social approach to "redefining" and re-orienting the reader to the sacrosanct place that the family occupies in every generation and the need to approach role and involvement. In the family, we look towards the next generation with a focus on diligent stewardship.

The author ushers his readers into the depths of the Divine blueprint for the family, how to build strong marriages while raising godly children. He proposes tremendous tenets for stewardship and financial wisdom with special reference to the family and shows the reader what it takes to invest in generational wealth within the faith context in an attempt to preserve the legacy of every family. Granted that marriage and family are so strategic in God's scheme of things to the fulfilment of His purposes in every generation, challenges and trials will often hit this institution. Dr Rolls makes a powerful presentation of how to navigate these when they show their ugly head in order to preserve the sanity of the family.

The book is an amazing manual for families, relationship and marriage counsellors/family therapists, finance experts, the clergy, social workers, and actors from other walks of life. Dr Rolls presents an amazing contextual definition of the concept of "wealth", anchored on the biblical mandate of "Be fruitful and multiply and replenish the earth". He puts a powerful accent on the stewardship role that each member of the family owes their creator, who is the owner of all, with emphasis that for succession to be effective, each generation needs to do their own homework in a bid to not only generate but also preserve and transfer its wealth to the ensuing one.

Though the author places clear emphasis on family life in this book from a Christian perspective, it is worth-noting that the principles and precepts he proposes cut across diverse cultures, religious orientations as well as generational settings. If carefully comprehended and practiced, the content of this book is capable of reshaping our society beginning with family life and passing across powerful and impact-driven values and virtues from generation to generation.

THIS BOOK IS A MUST! Get a copy, read it, re-read it and practice its content to write your name on the list of contributors to the greatness of the family in your time and beyond.

Rev. Tatoh Kenneth
Author, Relationship and Marriage Counsellor, Leadership Expert

Table of Contents

Introduction

In today's fast-paced world, where materialism often precedes spiritual values, Christians must revisit and reflect upon the principles that guide our faith and family life.

We come from a time when staunch Christians frowned upon the generation of wealth, as they were made to believe that Money was the root of all evil. Missionaries of the past made this into a Gospel, and because many of our believers did not read the scriptures for themselves, they believed it as they heard it.

As I was busy studying and doing my research on this book, I looked back at how we were taught as Catholics and altar boys. We would listen to preachings and teachings that money was evil and that one could not serve God and Money. This caused us to believe that anything we did must not be about the generation of financial wealth. We believed that we could generate all the great things without financial wealth and freedom, as money was evil.

I realise today that the credit system was created so people could acquire everything they needed without having the money to buy them by taking them on credit. Proverbs 22:7 warns, "The borrower is a slave to the lender." Managing and reducing debt is a biblical principle that can help secure financial stability and prevent future generations from being burdened by excessive debt.

Seeking wise counsel, both in financial matters and life decisions, is a biblical practice. Financial planning and seeking godly advice can lead to generational financial success. Proverbs 15:22 advises,

"Plans fail for lack of counsel, but with many advisers, they succeed."

When rooted in biblical principles, generational wealth extends far beyond monetary riches. It encompasses the invaluable inheritance of faith, wisdom, and values that we pass down to our children and their children, creating a lasting legacy that reflects God's grace and love.

The Bible is a timeless source of wisdom that provides us with invaluable guidance on how to build strong foundations for our faith and family life. It teaches us about the importance of stewardship, the value of hard work, the significance of honouring God with our finances, and the role of faith in our daily lives.

Throughout the Bible, we find stories of individuals and families who faced trials and tribulations yet remained faithful to God. Their stories serve as powerful examples of how our faith can sustain us through the challenges of life and how our families can be a source of strength and support.

As followers of Christ, we are called to be good stewards of the resources God has entrusted to us. This extends beyond mere financial management; it encompasses the nurturing of our relationships, the cultivation of a strong foundation of faith, and the commitment to leaving a godly heritage for our descendants.

Our faith in God and our commitment to our families are intertwined, forming a strong and stable base upon which we build our lives. Hebrews 11:6 reminds us that without faith, it is impossible to please God. Our faith is not just a set of beliefs but a personal, trusting relationship with God through Jesus Christ. It provides us with guidance, hope, and the assurance of eternal life. This faith influences decisions, handling challenges, and treating others.

The family is a divine institution created by God. It is the basic building block of society. God's plan for the family is outlined in Ephesians 5:22-33 and Colossians 3:18-21, emphasising mutual love, respect, and submission among family members. The family is where faith is nurtured and passed down through generations.

Parents play a crucial role in nurturing their children's faith. Proverbs 22:6 instructs us to "Train up a child in the way he should go; even when he is old, he will not depart from it." This means that parents are responsible for teaching their children about God, His Word, and the principles of Christian living.

The foundation of faith and family is built on a deep and abiding trust in God, with our families as the primary arena for living out our faith. It involves nurturing our faith, passing it down to the next generation, and supporting one another in our spiritual journeys. Through this foundation, we seek to honour God, strengthen our families, and be a light to the world, reflecting the love of Christ in all we do.

A biblical guide to generational wealth is a profound journey through the wisdom and principles found in the Bible. It can help individuals and families manage their financial resources in a way that honours God and leaves a lasting legacy for future generations.

The Bible teaches us that everything we have belongs to God, and we are called to be faithful stewards of His resources. This concept is exemplified in the Parable of the Talents (Matthew 25:14-30), where individuals are entrusted with different amounts and are expected to invest them wisely. This parable emphasises the importance of responsible financial management.

Proverbs 10:4 states, "Lazy hands make for poverty, but diligent hands bring wealth." The Bible encourages us to work diligently and be responsible financially. Diligence and hard work are essential to building wealth that can be passed down to future generations.

Generosity is a core biblical principle. 2 Corinthians 9:11 tells us that we are enriched in every way to be generous in every way. As we accumulate wealth, we are called to be generous with our resources, not only to bless others but also to teach our children the importance of giving.

Deuteronomy 6:6-7 encourages parents to teach God's commandments diligently to their children. This includes imparting financial wisdom, budgeting, and responsible money management skills to the next generation.

While earthly wealth is important, the Bible reminds us of the greater treasure of eternal life with God. Jesus said, "Do not store up for yourselves treasures on earth, where moths and vermin destroy, and where thieves break in and steal. But store up for yourselves treasures in heaven" (Matthew6:19-20). A biblical guide to generational wealth emphasises the eternal significance of our financial choices.

Incorporating these biblical principles into our financial practices can help us build and preserve wealth that extends beyond our lifetimes. It's not merely about accumulating riches but doing so in a way that aligns with God's will and benefits our families and communities. By following these biblical guidelines, we can leave a legacy of faith, responsible stewardship, and generosity that honours God and blesses future generations.

I believe that as you read this book, you will be inspired and will apply these teachings to your family life. I only wish for you that you may prosper in all aspects of your life and see this as a tool to begin or improve on your journey to creating a lasting legacy and generational wealth for your family.

1|The Divine Blueprint for Family

Understanding God's design for the family is a foundational and deeply spiritual aspect of our faith journey as Christians.

The family unit is a divine institution God established from the beginning of creation. **Genesis 2:24** reads, "Therefore a man shall leave his father and his mother and hold fast to his wife, and they shall become one flesh." This verse reveals God's intention for marriage and the family.

God's design for the family reflects His love and order. Within the family, we learn valuable lessons about love, sacrifice, forgiveness, and faith. As followers of Christ, we are called to honour and uphold the sanctity of the family unit. This means striving for strong, loving marriages and nurturing our children in a way that aligns with the teachings.

The Bible provides us with guidance on various aspects of family life. For example, **Ephesians 5:22-25** instructs husbands to love their wives as Christ loved the church and wives to submit to their husbands in love and respect. Parents are encouraged to raise their children in the instruction and discipline of the Lord **(Ephesians 6:4).**

These verses tell us that God's design for the family is built upon love, respect, and mutual submission.

Furthermore, the family serves as a microcosm of the Church, where we learn to love and support each other in need and grow in our faith together. It is a place where we can experience God's grace and redemption through our relationships and a context in which we can fulfil our roles as spouses, parents, and children in a way that brings glory to God.

In today's world, where the concept of family is often challenged and redefined, Christians must hold fast to God's design for the family. We should pray for wisdom and guidance in our family lives, seek reconciliation and forgiveness when conflicts arise, and prioritise the spiritual growth of our loved ones. By doing so, we honour God's plan and create a nurturing environment where faith can flourish and God's love can be experienced daily.

It reminds us of His wisdom, love, and intention for our lives. As we embrace and live out these principles in our families, we become a testimony to the world of God's goodness and grace, and we contribute to building a society that values and upholds the sanctity of the family unit. When a family is built, it is built on the sole fact that it would be protected and loved and cherished, and hence, I believe that when we read the scripture **Genesis 2:24**, "Therefore a man shall leave his father and his mother and hold fast to his wife, and they shall become one flesh."
As I read this scripture and looked deep into it, I saw a three. I saw a Date Tree in my head.

The Importance of Family in Scripture

Family holds a central place in Scripture, and its importance is woven throughout the Bible's teachings and narratives. Understanding the significance of family in the context of our faith helps us appreciate the divine plan God has for us as individuals and as part of a larger community.

As stated above, the book of Genesis establishes the very foundation of the family. God created Adam and Eve, the first human couple, and blessed them, saying, "Be fruitful and multiply and fill the earth" **(Genesis 1:28).** This divine blessing highlights the sacredness of marriage and family as a means to fulfil God's purpose on Earth.

Throughout the Old Testament, we see the importance of family in the context of God's covenant with His people. God made covenants not only with individuals like Abraham but also with their descendants. These covenants often extended blessings and promises to future generations, emphasising the interconnectedness of families in God's plan.

The Bible repeatedly emphasises the role of parents in teaching and training their children in the ways of the Lord. **Proverbs 22:6** tells us, "Train up a child in the way he should go; even when he is old, he will not depart from it. This underscores the responsibility of parents to impart faith and values to their offspring.

The New Testament further highlights the importance of family relationships. In **Ephesians 5,** husbands are called to love their wives as Christ loved the church, and wives are encouraged to submit to and respect their husbands. These teachings emphasise the sacrificial love and mutual respect that should characterise family life. The Bible also emphasises the importance of caring for family members in need. **1 Timothy 5:8** states, "But if anyone does not provide for his relatives, and especially for members of his household, he has denied the faith and is worse than an unbeliever." This underscores the duty of family members to support and care for one another.

The New Testament prevalently describes the Church as the family of God. Believers are called brothers and sisters in Christ, and the Church serves as a spiritual family where believers find fellowship, support, and accountability.

The importance of family in Scripture is deeply rooted in God's design for humanity. It serves as a vehicle for passing on faith, values, and love from generation to generation. As Christians, we are called to honour and nurture our families, recognising that they are a gift from God and a reflection of His love and care for us. By doing so, we strengthen our families and contribute to the flourishing of our faith communities and society.

Building on a Strong Foundation

Jesus Christ, in His teachings, illustrated this principle through the parable of the wise and foolish builders, as recorded in the Gospel of **Matthew 7: 24-27**

"Everyone then hears these words of mine and does them will be like a wise man who built his house on the rock. And the rain fell, and the floods came, and the winds blew and beat on that house, but it did not fall because it had been founded on the rock, and everyone who hears these words of mine and does not do them will be like a foolish man who built his house on the sand. And the rain fell, and the floods came, and the winds blew and beat against that house, and it fell, and great was the fall of it."

This parable illustrates the importance of not only hearing the teachings of Jesus but also putting them into practice. The rock represents a solid foundation, which is a life built upon faith in Christ and obedience to His Word. Such a foundation provides stability and resilience in the face of life's storms. The foundation of our faith is a personal relationship with Jesus Christ. Believing in Him as our Savior and Lord is the bedrock upon which everything else is built.

The Bible is our guide and source of spiritual nourishment. Regular study and meditation on God's Word help us grow in wisdom and understanding. Prayer is our direct line of communication with God. Building a strong prayer life strengthens our relationship with Him and aligns our will with His. Being part of a faith community, such as a church, provides support, accountability, and opportunities for service and growth. Serving others, motivated by love and a desire to follow Christ's example, is a cornerstone of the Christian life. Pursuing a life of holiness and righteousness through the power of the Holy Spirit is essential for building a strong foundation. Sharing our resources and blessings with others reflects God's love and grace.

By building our lives upon these principles, we create a firm foundation that can withstand the trials and challenges of life. It's important to remember that while storms may come, our faith and obedience to Christ provide the strength and resilience needed to endure and emerge stronger on the other side.

As Christians, we are called to continually build and strengthen our foundation in Christ, knowing that it not only benefits us personally but also allows us to be a light source of hope to others in a world often buffeted by storms of various kinds.

The Symbolism of Date Trees

A Reflection of Family Structure and Reproduction

I introduced my thinking earlier in this chapter and now would like to sum it all up for you. Genesis 2: 24 represents a Date tree whose similarities reflect so much of a family. I would align this throughout the book where relevant.

In nature, the date tree stands as a remarkable example of growth, reproduction, and the perpetuation of life. By examining the life cycle and reproductive process of date trees, we can draw intriguing parallels to the structure of the family unit as described in scripture. This essay aims to explore the symbolic connection between the growth and fruit-bearing of date trees and the biblical concept of leaving one's parents to form a new family unit.

The Life Cycle and Reproduction of Date Trees

Date trees (Phoenix dactylifera) are dioecious, meaning they have separate male and female trees. To produce fruit, the male and female trees must be merged. The male tree produces clusters of flowers called inflorescences, while the female tree bears the fruit. However, they cannot self-pollinate; rather, they rely on the assistance of wind or insects to facilitate the transfer of pollen from the male flowers to the female flowers. This cross-pollination process ensures the propagation of the species.

Symbolism of Date Trees in Relation to Family Structure

The parallel between the reproductive process of date trees and the biblical concept of family structure is striking. In **Genesis 2:24,** it is written, "Therefore a man shall leave his father and his mother and hold fast to his wife, and they shall become one flesh." Just as the male and female date trees merge to produce fruit, a man and a woman leave their respective families to form a new family unit bound together in marriage.

Leaving One's Parents

The process of leaving one's parents is a crucial step in the formation of a new family. It signifies a transition from dependence to independence and a commitment to forge a new path together. Similarly, when the male and female date trees are planted separately, they grow independently and establish their own roots. However, once they are brought together, they intertwine, supporting one another's growth and well-being.

Becoming One Flesh

When a man and a woman unite in marriage, they become one flesh. This unity is not merely physical but extends to emotional, spiritual, and intellectual levels. Similarly, when the male and female date trees are merged, they create a harmonious union that allows them to fulfil their purpose of producing fruit. The interdependence of the trees exemplifies the unity and collaboration necessary for a successful family unit. **Reproduction and Legacy:** As the merged date trees grow, they not only continue to bear fruit themselves but also produce offshoots, which can be replanted to create new trees. This cycle of growth and reproduction ensures the continuity of the species. In a similar vein, within the family structure, the couple's union may result in the birth of children who carry on their legacy and perpetuate the family lineage.

Conclusion

The symbolism of date trees provides a profound insight into the beauty and significance of family structure. The merging of male and female trees, the process of leaving one's parents, the unity of becoming one flesh, and the cycle of reproduction and legacy all reflect the biblical principles guiding the formation and growth of a family. By recognising the intricate parallels between nature and scripture, we can appreciate the divine harmony that exists within the world around us and the wisdom encapsulated in ancient texts.

2|Building Strong Marriages

This is a fundamental aspect of Christian life and reflects the divine plan for human relationships as outlined in the Bible.

The institution of marriage is sacred, and it is a covenant designed by God to be a source of love, support, and spiritual growth.

The foundation of a strong Christian marriage is a shared faith in Jesus Christ. Both spouses should prioritise their relationship with God individually and as a couple. Centering the marriage on Christ provides a solid foundation upon which to build.

Effective communication is essential in any relationship, and marriage is no exception. Open, honest, and loving communication fosters understanding, trust, and intimacy between spouses. Ephesians 4:2-3 encourages us to "Be completely humble and gentle; be patient, bearing with one another in love. Make every effort to keep the unity of the Spirit through the bond of peace."

Christian love is characterised by selflessness and sacrificial love. **Philippians 2:3-4** teaches us to "do nothing out of selfish ambition or vain conceit. Rather, in humility, value others above yourselves, not looking to your own interests but each of you to the interests of the others."

Putting your spouse's needs and well-being above your own strengthens the marital bond.

Forgiveness is a cornerstone of our faith. In marriage, extending forgiveness and grace to one another is essential, just as Christ forgives us. **Colossians 3:13** reminds us to "Bear with each other and forgive one another if any of you has a grievance against someone. Forgive as the Lord forgave you."

Regularly seeking God's guidance and wisdom through prayer as a couple promotes unity and helps in decision-making and problem-solving. **James 5:16** encourages us to: **"Pray for each other so that you may be healed."**

This I can relate to very well, and as I bring it out here, I am reminded of when my marriage was going through a very troublesome period, and we were facing hard times in our faith and spirit; we were on the verge of going for divorce, but God and how we were able to overcome through. What worked for us was prayer. We prayed more, especially my wife. My wife became the warrior in our marriage. She took over the war room and became commander-in-chief, and when I saw how she was praying, I had no choice but to do the same.

At first, I was praying to take back the command centre as the head of the house, but as things went on, it was about restoring my family and marriage. Things started to turn around in our marriage; we saw each other differently and started handling problems together, and the team was rebuilt.

Therefore, I can attest to the power of praying for each other and its impact on your marriage. Through constant prayer, our marriage and family have been healed. **Ephesians 5:33** instructs husbands to love their wives and wives to respect their husbands. Mutual respect and honour in marriage strengthen the emotional and spiritual bonds.

Marriage is a lifelong commitment. Christians are called to honour their marriage vows and remain steadfast in their commitment to one another through all seasons of life.

If challenges arise that threaten the marriage, seeking counsel from a trusted Christian advisor, pastor, or marriage counsellor can be beneficial. **Proverbs 11:14** reminds us that "Where there is no guidance, a people falls, but in an abundance of counsellors, there is safety."

Building a solid Christian marriage is an ongoing journey that requires dedication, love, and a continual reliance on God's grace and guidance. When both spouses are committed to these principles, they can create a marriage that reflects God's love and serves as a testament to His faithfulness.

The Covenant of Marriage

The covenant of marriage is a sacred and profound concept deeply rooted in the Biblical teachings. It represents far more than a legal or social contract; it is a divine covenant ordained by God Himself. Understanding the covenant of marriage from a Christian perspective is crucial for appreciating its significance and enduring commitment.

As explained in chapter one, God established marriage in the Garden of Eden when He created Adam and Eve. **Genesis 2:24** highlights the divine intention for marriage as a union between one man and one woman.

In **Ephesians 5:31-32,** the Apostle Paul reveals that marriage is a profound mystery that points to the relationship between Christ and the Church. Christ's sacrificial love for the Church is mirrored in the love and selflessness that should characterise the husband-wife relationship.

Unlike a contract, which is based on mutual benefits, a covenant is based on unconditional commitment and promises. Christian marriage is a covenant before God and involves a lifelong commitment to love, honour, and cherish one another, for better or worse, in sickness and in health, until death parts the couple.

Christian marriage is a reflection of God's love for His people. Husbands are called to love their wives as Christ loved the Church, and wives are called to respect and submit to their husbands **(Ephesians 5:22-33).** This mutual love and respect mirror the love and reverence we have for God.

One of the purposes of marriage is to be fruitful and multiply, not only in terms of physical offspring but also in spiritual growth. A Christian marriage provides an environment for nurturing faith and passing on godly values to the next generation.

Ecclesiastes 4:9-12 says, "Two are better than one because they have a good return for their labour... Though one may be overpowered, two can defend themselves."

Christian marriage provides companionship, emotional support, and a partnership in facing life's challenges. The covenant of marriage includes the call to fidelity and purity. **Hebrews 13:4** reminds us, **"Let marriage be held in honour among all, and let the marriage bed be undefiled."** This underscores the importance of faithfulness and sexual purity within the marital relationship. Christian couples are encouraged to pray together and seek God's guidance as they navigate their marital journey. Unity in prayer strengthens the bond between spouses and invites God into the centre of the marriage.

The covenant of marriage in Christianity is a sacred and lifelong commitment that reflects God's love, grace, and faithfulness. It is a divine institution designed to bring glory to God through the loving and sacrificial relationship between a husband and wife. When couples embrace the covenantal nature of marriage, they can experience the joy and fulfilment that come from aligning their relationship with God's design.

Roles and Responsibilities in Marriage

In Christian marriage, roles and responsibilities are often guided by the teachings of the Scriptures. These roles are not about asserting authority or dominance but are based on love, mutual respect, and servant-hood principles.

Understanding and embracing these roles can lead to a harmonious and God-honoring marriage.

Husband's Roles

Understanding and embracing these roles with humility, love, and a servant's heart is essential, as they reflect the example set by Jesus Christ in His relationship with the Church. Here are some key roles and responsibilities of a husband in a Christian marriage:

- **Spiritual Leader: Ephesians 5:23** states that the husband is the head of the wife, just as Christ is the head of the Church. This does not imply dominance but rather spiritual leadership. Husbands are called to take responsibility for the spiritual well-being of their family. This includes leading in prayer, studying God's Word together, and setting an example of faith and devotion.

- **Selfless Love: Ephesians 5:25** instructs husbands to love their wives as Christ loved the Church. Christ's love for the Church was sacrificial, unconditional, and selfless. Husbands are called to prioritise their wives' well-being, happiness, and spiritual growth, even to the point of being willing to make personal sacrifices for their wives.

- **Provider and Protector:** Husbands are responsible for providing for their wives' and children's physical and emotional needs. This includes financial support, ensuring the family's safety, and creating a loving and secure environment. Just as Christ protects and cares for His Church, husbands are called to protect and provide for their families.

- **Honour and Respect: Ephesians 5:33** emphasises the importance of husbands lovingly and respectfully leading their wives. This means valuing their opinions, seeking their input, and treating them with dignity and honour. Husbands should avoid any form of demeaning or abusive behaviour.

- **Communication:** Effective communication is vital in marriage. Husbands should actively listen to their wives, share their thoughts and feelings, and work together to make decisions. Communication fosters understanding and unity in the marital relationship.

- **Fidelity: Hebrews 13:4** reminds husbands to honour the marriage covenant by remaining faithful and pure within the marriage. Fidelity is not only a commitment to sexual purity but also to emotional and relational faithfulness.

- **Parenting:** Husbands are equally responsible for the upbringing of their children. This includes providing guidance, discipline, and a loving example to their children. They should partner with their wives to ensure the children's physical, emotional, and spiritual well-being.

- **Prayer and Spiritual Growth:** Couples are encouraged to pray together and seek spiritual growth as a team. Husbands should lead by example in pursuing a deeper relationship with God and encouraging their wives in their faith journey.

The role of a husband in a Christian marriage is one of servant leadership, love, and sacrificial devotion. It involves caring for the family's spiritual, emotional, and physical needs while fostering an atmosphere of love, honour, and mutual respect. Ultimately, the goal is to mirror Christ's love for His Church and create a strong, thriving Christian marriage that glorifies God. As husbands, we know and understand the value of family; as in Africa, a man is not complete until he is married, and a family is incomplete without children. However, that alone does not reflect the husband in our African context; what reflects a husband is how you treat your wife and children. How you raise those children and their behaviour reflects on you and who you are.

Also, your wife's appearance must improve since you married her and must show that she is well taken care of. This, too, shows that husbands must be seen as good not only by their wives but also by society.

Wife's Roles

In Christian marriage, the roles and responsibilities of a wife are deeply rooted in biblical teachings that emphasise love, mutual respect, and partnership within the marital relationship. These roles are meant to create a harmonious and God-honoring marriage. Here are some key roles and responsibilities of a wife in a Christian marriage:

- **Supportive Partner: Ephesians 5:22-24** teaches wives to submit to their husbands as to the Lord. This submission is not about inferiority but is a recognition of the husband's role as the spiritual leader in the family. It involves supporting and respecting his decisions aligning with God's principles.

- **Helper and Nurturer:** Wives often play a central role in creating a loving and nurturing environment within the home. They are responsible for the emotional and relational aspects of the family, fostering an atmosphere of care, warmth, and hospitality.

- **Respect and Encouragement: Ephesians 5:33** emphasises the importance of wives respecting their husbands. Encouraging and affirming their husbands can help build their self-esteem and strengthen the marital bond. This respect is rooted in love and mutual honour.

- **Effective Communication:** Effective communication is vital in any marriage. Wives are encouraged to communicate openly, honestly, and lovingly with their husbands, sharing thoughts, concerns, and feelings. Good communication fosters understanding and unity.

- **Fidelity and Purity:** Just as husbands are called to faithfulness, wives are also called to remain faithful and pure within the marriage. **Hebrews 13:4** reminds us to honour the marriage covenant by maintaining emotional and physical fidelity.

- **Parenting:** Wives share the responsibility of parenting with their husbands. This involves providing guidance, discipline, and a loving example to their children. Working together as a team to raise children is essential for their physical, emotional, and spiritual well-being.

- **Prayer and Spiritual Growth:** Couples are encouraged to pray together and seek spiritual growth as a team. Wives can actively participate in spiritual activities, including attending church, studying the Bible, and praying with their husbands.

- **Self-Care:** Taking care of oneself physically, emotionally, and spiritually is important for a wife's well-being and her ability to fulfil her roles in the family. It allows her to be a source of strength and support to her husband and children.

- **Seeking God's Will Together:** Couples are called to seek God's guidance in their decision-making. Wives should actively participate in seeking God's will and working with their husbands to make decisions that align with biblical principles.

The role of a wife in a Christian marriage involves being a supportive, nurturing, and respectful partner who works alongside her husband to build a strong and God-honoring marital relationship. These roles are not about subjugation but about mutual love, honour, and cooperation, reflecting the love and unity of Christ and His Church.

Society views her through her husband's appearance, as his well-dressed look often leads to comments about how well his wife dresses him. This assumes she has a role in his clothing choices, highlighting that the wife reflects her husband's love and care, just as he reflects hers.

Mutual Responsibilities

In Christian marriage, mutual responsibilities form the foundation for a strong and harmonious relationship. These responsibilities are rooted in biblical principles and are designed to promote love, unity, and mutual support within the marital union. Here are some key areas of mutual responsibility in a Christian marriage:

- **Communication:** Effective communication is a shared responsibility. Both spouses are called to communicate openly, honestly, and lovingly with each other. This includes discussing concerns, making decisions together, and actively listening to each other's thoughts and feelings.
- **Spiritual Growth:** Couples are encouraged to grow spiritually together. This involves attending church together, studying the Bible as a team, and praying together. Nurturing each other's faith and seeking God's guidance in all aspects of life is a mutual responsibility.

- **Fidelity and Purity:** Both spouses are called to faithfulness and purity within the marriage. This includes emotional fidelity, sexual fidelity, and maintaining the sanctity of the marital covenant.
- **Parenting:** Raising children is a shared responsibility. Both husband and wife are responsible for providing guidance, discipline, and a loving example to their children. They should work together to ensure the children's physical, emotional, and spiritual well-being.
- **Financial Stewardship:** Managing finances is a mutual responsibility. Couples are encouraged to work together to create a budget, make financial decisions, and plan for the future. It is important to be good stewards of financial resources and avoid unnecessary debt.
- **Household Responsibilities:** Household chores and responsibilities should be shared equitably based on each spouse's strengths and availability. This promotes teamwork and ensures a balanced workload within the home.
- **Emotional Support:** Providing emotional support and encouragement to each other is a mutual responsibility. During times of joy and sorrow, both spouses should be there to uplift and comfort one another.
- **Conflict Resolution:** Handling conflicts and disagreements in a healthy and respectful manner is a shared responsibility. Couples should seek

resolution through communication and compromise and, when necessary, guidance from a trusted source, such as a counsellor or pastor.

- **Self-Care:** Taking care of oneself physically, emotionally, and spiritually is important for both spouses. It enables them to be the best versions of themselves within the marriage and contributes to the overall well-being of the family.
- **Prayer for Each Other:** Both spouses should pray for each other's well-being, growth, and spiritual journey. Praying for one another strengthens the marital bond and invites God into the centre of the marriage.
- **Seeking God's Will Together:** Couples are called to seek God's will in their decision-making. Together, they should actively seek His guidance and make decisions that align with biblical principles.

In a Christian marriage, these mutual responsibilities are based on love, respect, and the shared commitment to honour God in the marriage relationship. Embracing these responsibilities strengthens the marital bond and serves as a testimony of God's love and faithfulness to the world.

Just as the date trees produce offshoots that eventually become independent trees, parents are responsible for raising and nurturing their children, helping them develop their identities and abilities. **Proverbs 22:6** advises, "Train up a child in the way he should go; even when he is old, he will not depart from it." Parents are called to impart values, teach life skills, and guide their children's growth, ensuring they become productive and responsible individuals.

Therefore, in order to achieve this, both husband and wife must have a clear understanding of what they want and also have clear-set goals and objectives for how they want to raise their family together. This is what they must do to avoid any challenges in the future where they will pull in different directions.

Nurturing Love and Unity in Your Marriage

Nurturing love and unity in a Christian marriage is a sacred duty and a beautiful reflection of God's love for us. The Bible provides profound guidance on how couples can cultivate and maintain a strong and loving marital relationship based on principles of love, forgiveness, and unity. Here are some key ways to nurture love and unity in your marriage:

- **Prioritise God:** Make God the foundation of your marriage. Centre your relationship on Him, seeking His guidance, wisdom, and strength through prayer and Scripture. When both spouses have a deep, personal relationship with God, it creates a strong spiritual bond that underpins your marriage.
- **Effective Communication:** Open, honest, and loving communication is essential. Take time to listen to each other's thoughts, concerns, and feelings. Practice active listening and avoid

destructive communication patterns like blame or criticism. This is very important as explained earlier.

- **Quality Time:** Spend quality time together regularly. Quality time is about being fully present with each other, engaging in meaningful conversations, and enjoying shared activities. It reinforces your emotional connection.

- **Date Nights:** Continue dating each other even after marriage. Regular date nights can rekindle the romance and keep the spark alive in your relationship.

- **Forgiveness:** Forgiveness is a cornerstone of Christian love. Be quick to forgive and slow to anger. Remember that both spouses are imperfect and make mistakes. Just as Christ forgives us, extend forgiveness to each other. Buried grudges lead to bitterness, so effective communication is paramount.

- **Serve One Another:** Embrace a servant's heart. Seek opportunities to serve and support your spouse in their daily responsibilities. This selflessness fosters a loving and supportive environment.

- **Unity in Decision-Making:** Make decisions together as a team. Seek each other's input and work collaboratively to make choices that align with your shared values and goals.

- **Prayer Together:** Praying together as a couple can be a powerful way to strengthen your bond. Praying for each other's needs, concerns, and spiritual growth brings you closer to God and each other. Spouses that pray together, stick or stay together.

- **Shared Interests:** Find common interests and hobbies that you both enjoy. Shared activities create opportunities for bonding and making lasting memories.

- **Counsel and Support:** Seek counsel and support from trusted sources when needed. Whether it's a pastor, counsellor, or marriage mentor, seeking guidance during challenging times can help you navigate difficult situations.

- **Keep Romance Alive:** Continue to express love and affection for each other. Small gestures of love, like handwritten notes, affectionate words, and physical touch, can keep the romance alive.

- **Celebrate Milestones:** Celebrate your anniversary and other significant milestones in your marriage. Reflect on your journey together and express gratitude for the years you've shared.

Remember that nurturing love and unity is an ongoing process. Marriage requires intentional effort and commitment. By continuously seeking to grow in love, deepen your unity, and honour God in your relationship, you can build a strong, enduring, and God-honoring marriage that blesses both you and those around you.

Having a vision of your marriage is key to developing a vision statement, and both should believe in this vision and strive to achieve it.

3|Raising Godly Children

Raising godly children is one of the most significant responsibilities and blessings that Christian parents have. It is a calling to nurture and guide our children in ways that reflect God's love, truth, and grace.

Children learn by observing their parents. Modelling a Christ-like life, including honesty, humility, love, and compassion, is the foundation for teaching them about God. Regularly read and study the Bible together as a family. Share biblical stories, teachings, and principles that help your children understand God's character and His plan for their lives.

Foster a habit of family prayer. Praying together not only deepens your family's connection with God but also shows children the importance of seeking God's guidance and strength in all aspects of life.

Attend church services together and engage in family worship at home. Singing hymns, worship songs, and discussing sermons can help children grow in their understanding of worship and their relationship with God.

Create an environment where children feel comfortable asking questions about faith and spirituality. Address their doubts and inquiries with patience and biblical wisdom.

Encourage your children to apply their faith in

practical ways by serving others, showing kindness, and sharing their faith with their peers. Be active in community service and mission work as a family.

Foster a loving and respectful environment. Cultivate a loving and respectful atmosphere within your home. Encourage sibling harmony and model respect for one another, teaching children to treat others as they would like to be treated. Discipline is an essential aspect of child-rearing and should be done with love and a focus on teaching and correction rather than punishment. It helps children understand right from wrong and the importance of obedience.

Pay attention to your children's spiritual growth and encourage them to develop their unique gifts and talents for God's service. Provide resources and opportunities for them to grow spiritually.

Spend quality time with your children. Engage in their activities, interests, and concerns. Show them that you care about every aspect of their lives. Encourage them to have Christian friends and mentors who can reinforce their faith and values.

Teach your children about God's grace and forgiveness. Help them understand the concept of repentance and the importance of seeking forgiveness when they make mistakes. Continuously pray for your children's well-being, safety, and spiritual growth. Trust in God's sovereignty over their lives.

Raising godly children is a noble and sacred calling in Christendom. It involves nurturing and guiding our children in a way that helps them develop a deep and meaningful relationship with God and equips them to live out their faith in the world.

Children as a Heritage from the Lord

Children are indeed a precious gift and heritage from the Lord. This profound truth is beautifully expressed in Psalm 127:3, which says, "Behold, children are a heritage from the Lord, the fruit of the womb a reward."

As Christians, we recognize that every child is a unique and priceless blessing entrusted to us by God. This understanding has several important implications.

We are called to be faithful stewards of the precious gift of children. This means nurturing, loving, and guiding them in ways that honour God and promote their physical, emotional, and spiritual well-being.

Parents have a significant responsibility in raising children. Ephesians 6:4 instructs parents to discipline and instruct their children in the Lord. This involves teaching them God's ways, modelling a Christ-like life, and instilling biblical values.

Children thrive in an environment of love, care, and security. Just as God loves and cares for us, parents are called to provide a safe and loving home where children can grow and develop their unique God-given potential.

One of the most important aspects of parenting is nurturing a child's spiritual growth. Proverbs 22:6 encourages us to "Train up a child in the way he should go; even when he is old, he will not depart from it." This involves teaching them about God, praying, and leading them to a personal relationship with Jesus Christ.

Children often carry their parents' values, faith, and teachings into the future. Parents can leave a lasting legacy of faith and righteousness that extends to future generations by raising them in a godly and loving home.

Recognizing children as a heritage from the Lord reinforces the importance of the family unit in God's plan. Families are meant to be places of love, support, and spiritual growth where children are nurtured and prepared to live purposeful lives for God's glory.

Understanding that children are a gift from God leads to gratitude and humility. Parents acknowledge that they cannot control the number or nature of the children they receive; rather, they trust God's plan and providence.

Parents are encouraged to pray fervently for their children's well-being, protection, and salvation. Prayer is a powerful tool for seeking God's guidance and blessings in their lives.

Children are indeed a heritage from the Lord, a precious gift to be treasured, loved, and nurtured. As Christians, we are called to fulfil our roles as faithful stewards, responsible parents, and spiritual guides, raising our children to know and love the Lord. In doing so, we honour God's gift and contribute to the growth of God's kingdom on earth.

Discipline Your Children in the Ways of the Lord

Disciplining our children in the ways of the Lord is a sacred responsibility and a central aspect of Christian parenting. As parents, we are called to guide and nurture our children's spiritual growth, teaching them to love and follow Jesus Christ. Here are some key principles for disciplining children in the ways of the Lord.

Children learn by example. Our own faith and relationship with God serve as a powerful model for them. Demonstrating a personal, vibrant faith through prayer, Bible study, worship, and acts of service sets a strong foundation.

Regularly reading and studying the Bible together as a family is essential. Share age-appropriate Bible stories, discuss their meanings, and encourage questions. Deuteronomy 6:6-7 says, "These commandments that I give you today are to be on your hearts. Impress them on your children. Talk about them when you sit at home, walk along the road, lie down, and get up."

Teach your children the importance of prayer. Pray with them and encourage them to pray on their own. Share prayer requests, express gratitude, and seek God's guidance together as a family.

Engage in family worship times where you sing hymns and songs of praise and worship together. This fosters a sense of reverence and love for God.

We attended our Family Development Institute training in Ghana a few years ago with Dr. Abu Bako at the Logos Rhema Leadership Development Institute. There, we were taught about developing values in our children that would grow into a culture and tradition we wished to reflect in our families.

Upon our return, my wife and I decided to spend more time with our family. In doing so, we taught them about the scriptures and the love of God. We established that our responsibility was to guide our children to be grounded in the values we wanted to instill. We introduced daily prayers where we read Psalms every evening, selecting specific Psalms for them to learn and recite verbatim. We started with five Psalms and gradually added more, sometimes introducing scripture from the book of Corinthians.

I will share our chosen Psalms and scriptures and their meanings for our family later. We also introduced simple family rules that have become part of our family values.

We eat together at the dining table. Since we are a large family, I invested in a 12-seater table so we can all sit together. At the table, there are no phones or distractions like television; we use this time to share conversations and jokes. Dinner has become a time of fellowship in the house, and we treasure it.

Church is a family affair, and even visitors know we all attend church together. If we do not attend church, we have a family service at home where the children also get to share.

We should regularly attend church services as a family and actively participate in church activities and ministries. We should also encourage our children to join youth or children's groups where they can grow in faith alongside their peers.

Create an environment where your children feel comfortable discussing their faith, doubts, and questions. Address their inquiries honestly and sensitively, always pointing them toward biblical truth.

Teach biblical values and virtues such as love, kindness, forgiveness, and humility. Help your children apply these principles daily, emphasizing that living out their faith is as important as knowing it.

Involve your children in acts of service and outreach to others. Show them the importance of loving their neighbours and caring for those in need.

Discipline your children with love and consistency, using biblical principles of correction and instruction (Proverbs 22:6). Discipline should always be aimed at teaching and guiding them toward righteousness.

Welcome questions and doubts as opportunities for growth. Encourage your children to seek answers through prayer, Scripture, and discussions with trusted adults.

Provide age-appropriate Christian books, devotionals, and resources that reinforce faith and biblical values. These can be valuable tools for deeper understanding.

Lift your children in prayer daily, asking God to guide, protect, and shape their hearts according to His will.

Disciplining our children in the ways of the Lord is a lifelong journey that requires patience, prayer, and a deep commitment to their spiritual growth. As parents, we have the privilege and responsibility to nurture their faith, helping them develop a personal relationship with Jesus

Christ that will serve as a strong foundation for their lives.

Passing Down Faith and Values to the Next Generation

This involves imparting a deep and enduring understanding of God's love and biblical principles to our children. There are some essential strategies for effectively passing down faith and values.

Children often learn the most from what they see in their parents. Demonstrating a genuine, vibrant faith in your daily life serves as a powerful model for your children. As mentioned earlier, live out the values you want to instill, such as love, kindness, forgiveness, and integrity.

As mentioned earlier, regular family devotional times is an excellent way to study the Bible, pray, and discuss faith together.

Reading and reflecting on Scripture as a family deepens everyone's understanding and strengthens their connection to God.

4|Stewardship and Financial Wisdom

Stewardship and financial wisdom are central concepts in Christianity. They emphasise our responsibility to manage the resources God has entrusted us according to His principles and purposes.

Stewardship is the acknowledgement that all our possessions, talents, and resources ultimately belong to God. As stewards, we are called to manage these blessings faithfully, recognising that we are not owners but caretakers. This perspective shifts our focus from ownership to responsibility. As faithful stewards, we are entrusted with these resources to manage them responsibly and in a manner that honours God.

In Psalm 24:1, it is written, "The earth is the Lord's, and everything in it, the world, and all who live in it." This verse underscores the foundational belief that God is the Creator and Owner of everything. As stewards, we are caretakers of His creation.

Stewardship carries the responsibility of managing God's resources wisely. In the Parable of the Talents (Matthew 25:14-30), Jesus teaches that we will be held accountable for using the gifts and resources entrusted to us. This accountability extends to our time, talents, and finances.

It also involves sacrificial giving. In 2 Corinthians 9:6-7, we are reminded, "Whoever sows sparingly will also reap sparingly, and whoever sows generously will also reap generously." This principle encourages us to give generously, knowing that God blesses those who give with a willing heart.

Stewardship also includes contentment with what God has provided. In Philippians 4:11-12, the Apostle Paul writes, "I have learned to be content whatever the circumstances." Contentment helps us avoid the trap of materialism and find joy in God's provision.

Generosity is a key aspect of stewardship. As stewards of God's blessings, we are called to be generous with our resources, not only in terms of financial giving but also in sharing our time, talents, and love with others.

2 Corinthians 9:7 encourages us to give cheerfully, reflecting a heart of gratitude.

Stewardship extends to serving others. Galatians 5:13 reminds us, "Serve one another humbly in love." Our stewardship should manifest in acts of service and kindness toward our fellow human beings. Christian stewardship includes a focus on eternal treasures. Jesus advises us in Matthew 6:19-20, "Do not store up for yourselves treasures on earth, where moths and vermin destroy, and where thieves break in and steal. But store up for yourselves treasures in heaven." This emphasises the eternal value of our actions and investments.

By embracing the principles of stewardship, Christians seek to honour God with their lives and leave a lasting impact on His kingdom. Financial wisdom involves making sound and prudent decisions about one's finances.

The Bible is replete with wisdom on this subject, such as Proverbs 21:5, which states, "The plans of the diligent lead to profit as surely as haste leads to poverty."

Financial wisdom encourages us to plan, budget, and make informed financial choices.

1 Timothy 6:10 warns, "For the love of money is a root of all kinds of evil." Christians are cautioned against making money an idol in their lives. Maintaining a healthy perspective on wealth and prioritising our relationship with God above material possessions is essential.

Generosity is a key element of stewardship and financial wisdom. 2 Corinthians 9:7 reminds us, "Each of you should give what you have decided in your heart to give, not reluctantly or under compulsion, for God loves a cheerful giver." Giving to support God's work and help those in need is a reflection of a wise and generous heart.

Proverbs 22:7 advises, "The rich rule over the poor, and the borrower is slave to the lender." Wise financial stewardship includes managing and reducing debt to avoid undue financial burdens and maintain financial freedom.

Proverbs 15:22 says, "Plans fail for lack of counsel, but with many advisers, they succeed." Seeking godly financial advice and counsel from trusted individuals can provide valuable insights and prevent costly mistakes.

Contentment is an essential aspect of financial wisdom. Philippians 4:11-12 says, "I have learned to be content whatever the circumstances." Learning to be content with what we have can lead to financial peace and help us avoid unnecessary spending.

Financial wisdom in Christianity involves recognising that our ultimate treasure is in heaven. Matthew 6:19-21 encourages us to store up treasures in heaven, where they are secure and everlasting.

This perspective helps us prioritise eternal wealth over temporary riches.

Stewardship and financial wisdom go hand in hand for Christians. By living out these principles, we not only manage our finances well but also honour God in our financial choices, ultimately leading to a life of greater purpose and fulfilment.

God's Ownership and Our Stewardship

Understanding the concept of God's ownership and our stewardship is a fundamental aspect of our faith that shapes how we view our lives, possessions, and responsibilities. We are called to manage His resources faithfully.

Psalm 50:10-12 declares, "For every animal of the forest is mine, and the cattle on a thousand hills. I know **every bird in the mountains and the insects in the fields are mine. I would not tell you if I were hungry, for the world is mine and all that is in it." These verses emphasise God's sovereignty as the Creator and Owner of everything.**

Stewardship is the divine assignment given to humanity. Genesis 1:26-28 teaches that God entrusted humanity with dominion over the earth and its resources. We are caretakers responsible for managing God's creation according to His purposes.

It carries the weight of accountability. In the parable of the rich fool (Luke 12:16-21), Jesus warns against selfishness and materialism. The rich man in the parable is held accountable for focusing solely on his own wealth and not being rich toward God.

Recognising God's ownership leads to a spirit of giving and generosity. 2 Corinthians 9:11 reminds us, "You will be enriched in every way so that you can be generous on every occasion." We give not out of obligation but as an expression of gratitude for God's blessings.

Stewardship involves investing in God's kingdom work. Matthew 6:33 teaches, "Seek first his kingdom and his righteousness, and all these things will be given to you as well." We prioritise eternal values over temporal wealth.

Stewardship extends beyond financial resources to include the responsible use of our time and talents. 1 Peter 4:10 reminds us that we should use our gifts to serve others.

Recognising God's ownership and our stewardship is a transformative perspective that influences every aspect of our lives. It teaches us to be faithful managers of God's resources, live with accountability, embrace generosity, find contentment in Him, and invest in the eternal work of His kingdom. Ultimately, it leads us to a life that reflects God's love and priorities, seeking His glory above all else.

Biblical Principles of Financial Management

Biblical principles of financial management provide us with a solid foundation for handling our finances in a way that aligns with God's will and honours Him. These principles are derived from the teachings of the Bible and offer timeless wisdom for managing our resources.

God's Ownership and Stewardship

The foundational principle of biblical financial management is recognising that God is the ultimate owner of everything. Psalm 24:1 reminds us, "The earth is the Lord's, and everything in it, the world, and all who live in it." This perspective shifts our focus from ownership to stewardship, emphasising our responsibility to manage God's resources faithfully.

We are called to be faithful stewards in light of God's ownership. A steward is someone entrusted with the care and management of another's possessions. As Christians, we are stewards of the resources God has placed in our hands, which include our income, assets, and abilities, as earlier mentioned.

Stewardship involves accountability. We will ultimately give God an account of how we managed the resources He entrusted to us.

Recognising God's ownership leads to a willingness to give back to Him a portion of what we have received. This is seen in the practice of tithing, where believers give a tenth of their income to support God's work and demonstrate their acknowledgement of His ownership.

Malachi 3:10 encourages us to "Bring the whole tithe into the storehouse."

Beyond covenant practices, Christians are called to be generous and compassionate toward others. Acts of charity, helping those in need, and supporting causes that reflect God's heart for justice are expressions of our recognition of God's ownership and our desire to reflect His character.

Understanding God's ownership can also lead to contentment with what we have. 1 Timothy 6:6 tells us, "But godliness with contentment is great gain." When we realise that God provides for our needs and that our true wealth is found in Him, we can find contentment even in modest circumstances.

The principle of God's ownership helps us guard against materialism, the love of money, and the pursuit of wealth for its own sake. Instead, we prioritise our relationship with God and seek His guidance in our financial decisions.

Practising good financial planning, budgeting, and wise financial decisions are all part of being responsible stewards. Proverbs 21:5 states, "The plans of the diligent lead to profit as surely as haste leads to poverty." Planning aligns our financial management with God's purposes.

The biblical principle of God's ownership is a foundational concept in Christian financial management.

It reminds us that we are stewards, not owners and that our financial decisions should reflect our acknowledgement of God's sovereignty over all resources.

By living out this principle, we can manage our finances in a way that honours God, benefits others, and leads to financial peace and security.

Avoiding Debt

Proverbs 22:7 warns, "The rich rule over the poor, and the borrower is slave to the lender." Biblical wisdom encourages us to avoid excessive debt, which can lead to financial bondage. It reminds us that debt can lead to a form of servitude, limiting our financial freedom and independence. Managing debt responsibly is a vital aspect of financial stewardship.

Avoiding debt is a biblical principle of financial management. The Bible offers several verses and teachings that emphasise the importance of being cautious about debt and managing our financial affairs wisely.

Romans 13:8: In the New Testament, the Apostle Paul writes, "Let no debt remain outstanding, except the continuing debt to love one another, for whoever loves others has fulfilled the law." While this verse does not forbid all forms of debt, it explains the importance of fulfilling our financial obligations and not letting debt become a burden.

Proverbs 21:5: "The plans of the diligent lead to profit as surely as haste leads to poverty." This verse highlights the value of careful planning and diligence in financial matters. Rushing into debt without thoughtful consideration can lead to financial hardship.

Proverbs 6:1-5: In this passage, we find counsel

against making hasty financial commitments, especially when acting as a surety for someone else's debt. It warns of the potential consequences of such actions.

It's important to note that the Bible does not categorically forbid all forms of debt. There are instances where taking on debt may be a prudent financial decision, such as for purchasing an asset to resell for a large profit, investing to get a high ROI (Return on Investment), or in the case where you use property documents worth more than the amount loaned to you. However, the overarching principle is to exercise caution, be diligent in repayment, and avoid excessive or frivolous debt that can hinder our ability to serve God and provide for our families.

Biblical principles of financial management include avoiding debt as much as possible, practising prudent planning and diligence, and prioritising our relationship with God over material possessions. By following these principles, we can navigate our financial affairs in a way that honours God, promotes financial stability, and allows us to be more generous in our service to others.

Generosity

Generosity is a recurring theme in the Bible. 2 Corinthians 9:6-7 says, "Remember this: Whoever sows sparingly will also reap sparingly, and whoever sows generously will also reap generously. Each of you should give what you have decided in your heart to give, not reluctantly or under compulsion, for God loves a cheerful giver." Giving to support God's work and help those in need is a reflection of a generous and obedient heart.

The foundation of generosity in Christianity begins with recognising God's incredible generosity towards us. John 3:16 reminds us, "For God so loved the world that he gave his one and only Son, that whoever believes in him shall not perish but have eternal life." God's gift of salvation through Jesus Christ is the ultimate act of generosity, setting the example for how we should approach giving and generosity in our own lives.

It is a tangible way to demonstrate God's love to others. 1 John 3:17-18 urges us to help those in need and not withhold our resources when we have the means to help. Generosity is an expression of our faith and love in action. It should come from a willing and joyful heart, not out of obligation. When we give cheerfully, it not only blesses others but also brings joy and fulfillment to our own lives. The Bible often uses agricultural metaphors to illustrate the principle of sowing and reaping. Galatians 6:7 states, "Do not be deceived: God cannot be mocked. A man reaps what he sows." When we give generously, we are sowing seeds of blessings not only in the lives of others but also in our own lives. God promises to multiply our generosity.

In Matthew 6:19-20, Jesus instructs us to "Store up for yourselves treasures in heaven, where moths and vermin do not destroy, and where thieves do not break in and steal." Generosity is an investment in eternal treasures. Our acts of kindness, generosity, and helping those in need have eternal significance.

The early Christian community in Acts 2:44-45

exemplified generosity by sharing their possessions and resources with one another. Generosity extends to supporting the work of God's kingdom, including the church, missions, and charitable organisations that serve the needy.

Proverbs 11:25 reminds us, "A generous person will prosper; whoever refreshes others will be refreshed." Generosity benefits the recipients and brings blessings and refreshments to the giver.

Generosity is a vital biblical principle of financial management that flows from our understanding of God's love and grace. It involves giving with a cheerful heart, sowing seeds of blessings, and prioritising eternal treasures. As Christians, we are called to embody the generous nature of our Heavenly Father in our financial stewardship, knowing that by doing so, we not only bless others but also experience the abundant blessings of God in our own lives.

Planning and Budgeting

Proverbs 21:5 reminds us, "The plans of the diligent lead to profit as surely as haste leads to poverty." Creating a well-thought-out financial plan is a wise and responsible way to steward the resources God has given us. A budget and financial plan help us manage our resources effectively, avoid overspending, and prioritise our financial goals.

1 Timothy 6:6 advises, "But godliness with contentment is great gain." Contentment is a foundational principle for financial planning. It encourages us to be

satisfied with what we have and avoid excessive spending driven by discontent. Contentment allows us to allocate resources more wisely.

Budgeting is a practical application of financial planning. It involves allocating income to various expenses, savings, and giving systematically. Proverbs 24:27 says, "Prepare your work outside; get everything ready for yourself in the field; and after that, build your house." This verse highlights the importance of planning (preparing your work) before making significant financial commitments (building your house). Managing debt is a critical aspect of financial planning. A well-structured budget can help individuals avoid accumulating excessive debt and work toward becoming debt-free.

Proverbs 21:20 advises, "Precious treasure and oil are in a wise man's dwelling, but a foolish man devours it." Saving a portion of our income and establishing an emergency fund are prudent financial planning steps. They provide a safety net for unexpected expenses and help us build a foundation of financial stability.

Budgeting should include a category for giving generously. Proverbs 11:25 reminds us, "A generous person will prosper; whoever refreshes others will be refreshed." Including giving in our budget demonstrates our commitment to sharing our blessings with others.

In all our financial planning and budgeting, seeking God's guidance through prayer is essential. Proverbs 3:5-6 instructs us, "Trust in the Lord with all your heart and lean not on your own understanding; in all your ways submit to him, and he will make your paths straight." A fundamental principle is acknowledging God's wisdom and seeking His direction in financial matters.

By incorporating these principles into our financial practices, we can honour God with our finances, achieve financial stability, build generational wealth, and have the resources to bless others as well.

Contentment

Learning to be content with what we have is an essential principle of financial management. **Hebrews 13:5** says, "Keep your lives free from the love of money and be content with what you have because God has said, 'Never will I leave you; never will I forsake you.'" Contentment helps us avoid excessive consumption and materialism. It encourages us to find satisfaction and peace in God rather than in material possessions.

It is also important to note that being content should not be confused with accepting situations that we wish to change. Many times, Christians confuse being content with remaining unchanged; hence, we find people hallowing in poverty all in the name of being content. My understanding of being content is being satisfied with gradual development and not pushing for immediate results and chasing quick schemes that make us more focused on temporary changes but being content with stages of development and nurturing the gradual change as it comes and being content with where you are at that time knowing that no situation is are permanent.

A. Biblical Foundation of Contentment:

Contentment finds its roots in various passages throughout the Bible, such as:

Philippians 4:11-13: The Apostle Paul writes, "I have learned to be content whatever the circumstances. I know what it is to be in need, and I know what it is to have plenty. I have learned the secret of being content in any and every situation, whether well-fed or hungry, whether living in plenty or in want. I can do all this through him who gives me strength." This passage highlights the idea that true contentment comes from our relationship with Christ, not our external circumstances.

1 Timothy 6:6-8: "But godliness with contentment is great gain. For we brought nothing into the world, and we can take nothing out of it. But if we have food and clothing, we will be content with that." This passage underscores the idea that wealth is based on an individual's understanding and definition of wealth, and our primary focus should be on growing godliness and being content with life's essentials but never taking away the need to grow and create generational wealth.

B. Contentment in Financial Management:

Contentment in the context of financial management involves:

1. Avoiding Materialism: Contentment helps us resist the temptation of constantly pursuing more material possessions.

2. It allows us to be satisfied with what we have and not constantly strive for greater wealth or luxury.

3. Prudent Spending: Contentment helps us make wise spending decisions by distinguishing between our needs and wants. When we are content, we are less likely to engage in frivolous or impulsive spending.

4. Financial Peace: Cultivating contentment leads to financial peace. It reduces stress and anxiety associated with financial matters and allows us to trust God's provision.

5. Generosity: Content people are often more generous because the desire for more wealth does not drive them. They are willing to share their resources with others in need.

C. Practical Application

Practising contentment in financial management involves:

1. Gratitude: Regularly count your blessings and express gratitude for what you have. Gratitude shifts your focus from what you lack to what you've been given.

2. Setting Realistic Goals: While it's essential to have financial goals, ensure they are realistic and align with your needs and values rather than societal pressures.

3. Avoiding Comparison: Avoid comparing your financial situation with others. Comparison can lead to envy and discontentment.

4. Trust in God: Ultimately, contentment in financial management comes from trusting God as your provider. Recognise that He knows your needs and will take care of you.

By embracing contentment, we can find peace, make wise financial decisions, and prioritise our relationship with God over material possessions, leading to a more fulfilling and purposeful life.

Seeking Wise Counsel

Proverbs 15:22 advises, "Plans fail for lack of counsel, but with many advisers, they succeed." Seeking godly financial advice and counsel from trusted individuals can provide valuable insights and prevent costly mistakes.

The Bible is replete with verses emphasising the importance of seeking advice and guidance from knowledgeable and godly sources.

Proverbs 15:22: "Plans fail for lack of counsel, but with many advisers, they succeed." This verse from Proverbs highlights the critical role of seeking counsel when making financial decisions. It suggests that seeking input from others increases our chances of making wise and successful plans.

Proverbs 13:20: "Walk with the wise and become wise, for a companion of fools suffers harm." This verse explains the influence of our associations. It encourages us to surround ourselves with wise and godly individuals, especially financially, to avoid harmful consequences.

Proverbs 11:14: "For lack of guidance a nation falls, but victory is won through many advisers." While this verse primarily refers to leadership, it also applies to individual financial stewardship. Seeking advice from multiple advisers can lead to financial success and stability.

Proverbs 24:6 says, "Surely you need guidance to wage war, and victory is won through many advisers." Just as military leaders require counsel to achieve victory, individuals need wise counsel to navigate financial challenges and make sound decisions.

James 1:5: "If any of you lacks wisdom, you should ask God, who gives generously to all without finding fault, and it will be given to you." Ultimately, our first source of wisdom is God Himself. We are encouraged to seek His guidance through prayer and to trust that He will provide us with the wisdom we need.

Seeking Expertise: Seeking wise counsel also involves seeking out experts in financial matters, such as financial advisors, accountants, or legal professionals. These individuals can provide specialised knowledge and insights that can be invaluable in complex financial situations.

In addition to seeking financial advice, it's essential to have spiritual accountability. This can be in the form of a mentor, Pastor, or trusted friend who can provide guidance from a biblical perspective and hold you accountable for your financial decisions.

Incorporating the biblical principle of seeking wise counsel into financial management means recognising our need for guidance, humility in seeking advice, and discernment in choosing trustworthy advisers. It acknowledges that no one has all the answers and that seeking counsel aligns with God's design for community and shared wisdom.

As Christians, we are encouraged to seek counsel from worldly sources, the Word of God, and prayer. By combining God's wisdom with the guidance of godly advisers, we can make financial decisions that honour God, benefit our well-being, and ultimately contribute to our spiritual and financial growth.

Eternal Perspective

Biblical financial management encourages us to have an eternal perspective. **Matthew 6:19-21** reminds us to store up treasures in heaven, where they are secure and everlasting. This perspective helps us prioritise eternal wealth over temporary riches.

Biblical principles of financial management, grounded in an eternal perspective, provide invaluable guidance for Christians seeking to honour God with their finances.

In **Matthew 6:33,** Jesus instructs us, "Seek first his kingdom and his righteousness, and all these things will be given to you as well." Placing God's kingdom first in our financial decisions means aligning our spending, saving, and giving with His purposes.

Maintaining an eternal perspective means recognising that material wealth is temporary, but our actions and investments with an eternal focus have lasting significance. Our eternal investments include acts of love, service, and spreading the Gospel. These investments yield eternal rewards.

Seeking counsel and accountability from wise and godly advisors is a biblical practice **(Proverbs 15:22).** It helps ensure that our financial decisions align with God's principles. Incorporating these principles into our financial management leads to a life of purpose, stewardship, and a profound understanding of the eternal impact of our financial choices. By recognising that our resources are a gift from God and by managing them in alignment with His purposes, we not only honour Him but also experience greater financial peace and fulfilment.

Teaching Financial Responsibility to Your Children

This is not only a practical endeavour but also a vital aspect of raising them in the ways of the Lord. The Bible provides guidance on how parents can instil sound financial principles in their children's lives:

- Lead by Example: As parents, we must model good financial stewardship ourselves. Our children learn from observing our attitudes and behaviours toward money. Demonstrating responsible financial habits, such as budgeting, saving, and giving, sets a powerful example.

- Use Everyday Opportunities: Incorporate financial discussions into everyday life. When you shop together, explain budgeting choices. When you give to charity, involve your children in the decision and discuss why giving is important. These practical experiences can make financial concepts more tangible.

- Teach the Value of Work: Proverbs 22:6 instructs, "Train up a child in the way he should go; even when he is old, he will not depart from it." Teaching our children the value of hard work and the satisfaction of earning money through age-appropriate chores or part-time jobs can instil a strong work ethic.

- Budgeting and Saving: Introduce your children to budgeting and saving early on. Encourage them to set aside a portion of any money they receive, whether through allowances or gifts, for savings. Teach them the importance of setting financial goals.

- Avoiding Impulse Buying: Help your children understand the difference between needs and wants. Encourage them to think before making purchases and consider the long-term consequences of impulsive spending.

- Delayed Gratification: Teach the value of delayed gratification by discussing how saving for something they desire can be more rewarding than immediate spending. This principle can help instil patience and discipline.

- Generosity: Emphasise the importance of giving. Encourage your children to allocate a portion of their resources for charitable giving or helping others in need. This will teach them about the joy of generosity and fulfil the biblical principle of giving.

- Financial Literacy: As your children grow, provide age-appropriate lessons in financial literacy. Teach them about banking, interest, credit, and investing. Equip them with the knowledge they need to make informed financial decisions.

- Open Communication: Create an environment of open communication about money. Encourage your children to ask questions and seek guidance when making financial choices.

Be patient and supportive in addressing their financial concerns.

- Prayer and Faith: Encourage your children to seek God's guidance in their financial decisions. Teach them to pray about their finances and trust in God's provision.

Teaching financial responsibility to our children is about imparting practical skills and instilling biblical values and principles. By grounding their financial education in faith and wisdom, we equip them to navigate the complexities of money and finances while honouring God with their resources. **Proverbs 3:5-6** reminds us, "Trust in the Lord with all your heart and lean not on your own understanding; in all your ways submit to him, and he will make your paths straight." This includes our financial paths as well.

5|Investing in Generational Wealth

Investing in generational wealth involves financial planning and the cultivation of values, wisdom, and faith that can be passed down through the generations. It's about building a legacy that reflects God's principles and ensures the well-being of our descendants.

The foundation of generational wealth should be rooted in biblical principles. **Proverbs 13:22** states, "A good person leaves an inheritance for their children's children." This inheritance extends beyond material wealth to include spiritual and moral values.

Financial wisdom is one of the most valuable gifts we can pass on to the next generation. **Proverbs 22:6** advises, "Train up a child in the way he should go; even when he is old, he will not depart from it." This involves teaching financial responsibility, budgeting, and the importance of living within one's means.

Generosity is a cornerstone of Christian living. Teaching our children and grandchildren to be generous and compassionate toward others is a vital part of generational wealth. As **2 Corinthians 9:7** says, "Each of you should give what you have decided in your heart to give, not reluctantly or under compulsion, for God loves a cheerful giver."

Instilling a sense of contentment in our descendants is

essential for their financial well-being. **Philippians 4:11-12** reminds us that we can find contentment in Christ regardless of our circumstances. This contentment helps prevent the pursuit of materialism and debt.

Generational wealth goes beyond financial assets; it includes a spiritual legacy. Sharing our faith with our family and modelling a strong relationship with God is a priceless inheritance. **Psalm 78:4** emphasises the importance of passing down the stories of God's faithfulness to the next generation.

Proper estate planning is crucial for preserving generational wealth. This includes creating wills, trusts, and other legal instruments to ensure a smooth transition of assets and to minimise taxes and expenses.

Providing for our descendants' education and personal development is an investment in their future. This may include funding educational opportunities, vocational training, and personal growth experiences.

Healthy family relationships are a significant part of generational wealth. Investing time and effort in building strong family bonds and open communication can help preserve both financial and emotional wealth.

Throughout the process of building generational wealth, seeking God's guidance through prayer and discernment is essential. **Proverbs 3:5- 6** encourages us to trust the Lord with all our hearts and lean not on our own understanding, acknowledging Him in all our ways.

Investing in generational wealth as a Christian involves more than accumulating financial assets; it's about passing down values, wisdom, and faith that reflect God's love and principles. By intentionally incorporating these aspects into our financial planning and family life, we can leave a lasting legacy that honours God and benefits our descendants for generations.

Wealth as a Tool for God's Work

Wealth is often seen as a tool that God entrusts to us for His work and His purposes. It is not merely for our personal comfort or accumulation but for advancing God's kingdom and blessing others.

As Christians, we are called to be faithful stewards of the wealth and resources God has given us. This means recognising that God is the ultimate owner, and we are His managers. As explained earlier, we are accountable for how we use our wealth and resources. God calls us to be generous with our wealth. **2 Corinthians 9:11** informs us, "You will be enriched in every way to be generous in every way, which through us will produce thanksgiving to God." Generosity is a way of reflecting God's love and providing for those in need. Wealth can be a powerful tool for supporting ministries, missions, and charitable organisations doing God's work. Many churches and organisations rely on the financial contributions of believers to carry out their missions.

Wealth allows us to help those in need. **Proverbs 19:17** says, "Whoever is kind to the poor lends to the Lord, and he will reward them for what they have done." We fulfil a key aspect of our Christian calling by using our wealth to assist the less fortunate.

Wealth can be invested in activities and projects that advance God's kingdom, such as funding church-building projects, supporting Christian education, or promoting evangelistic efforts.

While wealth can be used for God's work, avoiding excessive materialism and living a simple and humble life is essential. **1 Timothy 6:7** reminds us that we brought nothing into this world, and we can take nothing out of it.

1 Timothy 6:10 warns that the love of money is the root of all kinds of evil. Christians are called to keep their priorities in check and not allow the pursuit of wealth to become an idol.

When using wealth for God's work, seeking God's guidance through prayer and discernment is crucial. **Proverbs 3:5- 6** encourages us to trust in the Lord with all our hearts and lean not on our understanding.

Wealth is a tool that God has entrusted to us for His purposes. It can support His work, help those in need, and advance His kingdom. However, it's essential to approach wealth with a humble and generous heart, recognising that it ultimately belongs to God. By using our wealth in alignment with God's will, we can make a meaningful impact in the lives of others and fulfil our Christian calling to be good stewards of God's blessings.

Leaving an Inheritance for Your Children's Children

It reflects the idea that, as Christians, we must provide for our immediate families and plan and work diligently to bless future generations. It's important to leave a legacy of blessing beyond our lifetime, as stated in Proverbs 13:22. It can be called a generational wealth verse. It states, "A good person leaves an inheritance for their children's children, but a sinner's wealth is stored up for the righteous."

To leave an inheritance for future generations begins with faithful stewardship. We are called to manage our resources wisely and in a way that honours God. This includes financial assets but also encompasses passing down spiritual values and a godly heritage.

While financial provision is essential, the spiritual inheritance we pass on is of even greater significance. Teaching our children and grandchildren about God's love, His Word, and the importance of faith is a priceless gift that can impact their lives for eternity.

Providing educational opportunities for future generations is a way to invest in their growth and success. This may involve setting up educational funds or encouraging a love for learning.

Encouraging generosity within the family is another way to leave a lasting inheritance. Teaching our descendants to be generous and compassionate toward one another and others reflects the values of Christ and can bring great blessings.

Sound financial planning, including estate planning, is crucial to ensure that assets are distributed according to our wishes and in a way that benefits our descendants.

While material provision is important, balancing material and spiritual inheritance is essential. Material wealth should not overshadow the legacy of faith and moral values.

Seek God's guidance and wisdom in your efforts to leave an inheritance for your children's children. Pray for wisdom and discernment in financial and family matters.

Leaving an inheritance for your children's children is a noble and biblical endeavour. It involves both material provision and the transmission of spiritual values.

Wisdom for Investment

Investing wisely is an important aspect of financial stewardship for Christians. While the Bible doesn't provide specific investment advice, it offers principles and wisdom to guide investment decisions.

- Prayerful Consideration: When making investment decisions, seek God's guidance through prayer. Pray for wisdom, discernment, and a clear understanding of your financial goals and values.

- Diversification: Diversify your investments to spread risk. Proverbs 21:20 advises, "The wise store up choice food and olive oil, but fools gulp theirs down." Similarly, diversifying your investments helps protect your financial well-being.

- Avoiding High-Risk Speculation: Avoid investments that involve excessive risk or speculation. Proverbs 13:11 warns, "Dishonest money dwindles away, but whoever gathers money little by little makes it grow." Steer clear of "get-rich-quick" schemes.

- Ethical Considerations: Ensure your investments align with your Christian values. Avoid supporting companies or industries that engage in practices contrary to your beliefs, such as gambling, tobacco, or weapons manufacturing.

- Stewardship: Approach investment as a form of stewardship. Recognise that your resources are ultimately God's, and you are responsible for managing them wisely.

- Long-Term Perspective: Adopt a long-term perspective when investing. Proverbs 21:5 reminds us, "The plans of the diligent lead to profit as surely as haste leads to poverty." Patient and disciplined investing can lead to financial growth over time.

- Risk Tolerance: Assess your risk tolerance and investment horizon. Everyone's financial situation and goals are different, so tailor your investment strategy to align with your specific circumstances.

- Professional Advice: Consider seeking advice from financial professionals or advisors who share your ethical and moral values. They can help you create an investment strategy that aligns with your financial goals and Christian principles.

- Avoiding Debt: Prioritise paying off high-interest debt before making significant investments. Proverbs 22:7 cautions against accumulating debt: "The rich rule over the poor, and the borrower is slave to the lender."

- Contentment: Cultivate contentment and avoid excessive materialism. 1 Timothy 6:6-7 reminds us, "But godliness with contentment is great gain. For we brought nothing into the world, and we can take nothing out of it." Contentment can lead to more responsible and thoughtful investment choices.
- Generosity: Continue to prioritise generosity and charitable giving, even as you invest. Proverbs 11:24-25 teaches, "One person gives freely, yet gains even more; another withholds unduly but comes to poverty."
- Monitoring and Adjusting: Review your investments regularly and adjust your strategy as needed to align with your goals and changing circumstances.

Remember that financial decisions, including investments, should be made in the context of your overall financial plan and with consideration of your long-term financial goals. Seek to balance the pursuit of financial growth with your Christian values and principles, always keeping in mind that stewardship and integrity should guide your financial decisions.

Financial Saving Strategy for Generational Wealth

This involves balancing the principles of stewardship, wisdom, and legacy building.

Seek God's Guidance: Begin by seeking God's guidance in your financial decisions. Pray for wisdom and discernment in managing your wealth with a focus on honouring God and benefiting future generations **(Proverbs 3:5-6)**.

Live Below Your Means: Practicing frugality and living below your means allows you to save and invest a significant portion of your income. This discipline can create a foundation for generational wealth **(Proverbs 21:20)**.

Create a Budget: Develop a budget that outlines your income, expenses, and savings goals. A budget helps you allocate funds toward saving and investing for the future **(Luke 14:28-30)**.

Save and Invest Wisely: Establish an investment strategy that aligns with your long-term financial goals. Diversify your investments to mitigate risk, and consider seeking advice from financial professionals **(Proverbs 21:5)**.

Teach Financial Literacy: Educate yourself and your children about financial literacy. Equip them with the knowledge and skills to manage wealth responsibly and make informed financial decisions **(Proverbs 13:22)**.

Include Charitable Giving: Integrate charitable giving into your financial plan. Generosity and giving to charitable causes are important aspects of Christian stewardship **(2 Corinthians 9:7)**.

Trust and Estate Planning: Consider creating a trust or estate plan to ensure the orderly transfer of assets to the next generation. Seek legal and financial advice to establish a plan that aligns with your values and goals **(Proverbs 13:22)**.

Set Clear Goals: Define your generational wealth

goals and objectives. Determine what you want to achieve and how you intend to provide for future generations, whether through education funds, inheritance, or other means.

Avoid Debt: Minimise or eliminate consumer debt, as it can hinder your ability to save and invest for the long term. **Proverbs 22:7** reminds us that "The borrower is a slave to the lender."

Regularly Review and Adjust: Periodically review your financial plan and make adjustments as needed. Economic conditions and personal circumstances can change, so adapt your strategy accordingly (Proverbs 27:23).

Generational Communication: Foster open and honest communication within your family about financial matters. Encourage conversations about your values, goals, and the responsibility of managing wealth.

Lead by Example: Model responsible financial stewardship and generosity for your children and heirs. Your actions can have a significant impact on their attitudes and behaviours regarding wealth management.

Pray for Wisdom: Continually seek God's wisdom and guidance in managing your wealth and making financial decisions. Trust that God will provide direction and bless your efforts **(James 1:5).**

Remember that the goal of generational wealth from a Christian perspective is not just accumulation for its own sake but using resources to honour God, support your family's needs, and make a positive impact on the world.

Generosity, wise stewardship, and faithfulness to biblical principles are key components of this financial strategy.

Financial Planning and Budgeting Template

Planning and budgeting are essential tools for managing your finances wisely and responsibly from a Christian perspective. Here's a template for creating a financial plan and budget that alignswith biblical principles:

1. Prayer and Reflection

Begin with prayer, seeking God's guidance and wisdom in yourfinancial planning **(Proverbs 3:5-6).**

Reflect on your financial goals and values, ensuring they align withyour Christian beliefs **(Proverbs 21:5).**

2. Income

List all sources of income, including salary, business income,investments, and any other sources.

3. Categorize your expenses:

Fixed expenses: *(e.g. rent/mortgage, utilities, insurance)*Variable expenses *(e.g. Groceries, transportation)* **Discretionary expenses:** *(e.g. entertainment, dining out)*

Charitable giving: *(e.g. tithe, offerings, and other charitable contributions)*

4. Financial Goals

Define your short-term and long-term financial goals, such as saving for emergencies, retirement, education, or charitable giving.

5. Savings and Investments

Allocate a portion of your income to savings and investments that align with your financial goals **(Proverbs 21:20)**.

6. Debt Management

List all outstanding debts, including credit card balances, loans, andmortgages. Develop a plan to manage and reduce debt, avoiding excessive borrowing **(Proverbs 22:7)**.

7. Generosity

Allocate a portion of your income for charitable giving, including your tithe and offerings **(Malachi 3:10)**.

8. Emergency Fund

Set aside funds for unexpected expenses or emergencies, such as medical bills or car repairs (Proverbs 21:20).

9. Review and Adjust

Regularly review your budget to track expenses and income. Make necessary adjustments to stay on track with your financial goals **(Proverbs 27:23)**.

10. Accountability

Consider sharing your financial goals and budget with a trusted friend, mentor, or accountability partner **(Proverbs 15:22)**.

11. Thanksgiving and Contentment

Cultivate an attitude of gratitude and contentment in your financialjourney **(Philippians 4:11-13)**.

12. Record Keeping

Maintain records of your income, expenses, and financial goals totrack progress over time.

13. Seek Professional Advice

If needed, consult with financial professionals, such as financial advisors or accountants, to ensure your financial plan is sound **(Proverbs 15:22)**.

14. Regularly Pray for Guidance

Continually seek God's guidance in your financial decisions and invite Him into your financial journey **(James 1:5)**. Our financial plan and budget should reflect our Christian values, including principles of stewardship, generosity, and responsible managementof resources. Regularly revisiting and adjusting our financial plan can help us align our finances with our faith and work towards financial stability and God-honoring goals.

Record Keeping

Record-keeping for generational wealth is essential to stewardship and responsible financial management. It involves maintaining accurate and organised financial records to ensure that wealth is effectively managed and can be passed down to future generations. The following are some key principles and steps for record-keeping:

- **Maintain Honesty and Integrity:** Begin with a commitment to honesty and integrity in all financial matters. Christians are called to be trustworthy stewards of the resources entrusted to them (Proverbs 11:3).

- **Create a Financial Inventory:** Develop a comprehensive financial inventory that includes all assets, liabilities, and investments. This inventory should cover bank accounts, real estate, stocks, bonds, retirement accounts, and any other valuable assets.

- **Organise Legal Documents: Ensure** that important legal documents, such as wills, trusts, and estate plans, are in place and up to date. Keep copies of these documents in a secure location, and provide necessary information to your heirs and designated representatives.

- **Document Income and Expenses:** Keep a record of all sources of income and detailed records of expenses. This includes tracking regular expenses, taxes, and any other financial obligations.

- **Investment Records:** Maintain records of all investments, including purchased amounts, purchase prices, and current values. Proper documentation helps with tracking investment performance and tax reporting.
- **Bank and Account Statements:** Keep copies of bank statements, investment account statements, and other financial account records. These documents provide a clear picture of financial transactions over time.
- **Tax Records:** Organise and retain tax records, including tax returns and supporting documentation, for the required number of years. Proper tax documentation is essential for compliance and potential audits.
- **Property and Real Estate Records:** Keep records related to property ownership, including deeds, titles, mortgage documents, and property appraisals. These documents may be crucial for future property transactions or inheritance.
- **Insurance Documents:** Maintain records of insurance policies, including life insurance, health insurance, and property insurance. Review and update coverage as needed.
- **Debt Records:** Document any outstanding debts, including loans, mortgages, and credit card balances. Include repayment schedules and terms.
- **Communication with Heirs:** Ensure that your heirs are informed about the location of important

financial records and documents. Maintain open and transparent communication about your financial plan and wishes for generational wealth.

- **Digital Records:** In today's digital age, consider digital record-keeping for added convenience and accessibility. Use secure digital storage solutions and ensure that trusted individuals have access to these records when necessary.

- **Regular Reviews:** Periodically review and update your financial records to reflect changes in your financial situation, such as new investments, acquisitions, or changes in beneficiaries.

- **Professional Guidance:** Consult with legal and financial professionals specialising in estate planning and wealth management. They can provide expert guidance on record keeping and estate administration.

Record-keeping for generational wealth helps ensure that our accumulated wealth can be used for the benefit of future generations by our values and goals. By maintaining organised and transparent records, we can contribute to the responsible transfer of wealth to our heirs and continue to honour God through our financial decisions.

6|Faith and Wealth

Faith is a fundamental aspect of one's relationship with God. It involves trust and belief in God's teachings, promises, and salvation through Jesus Christ. Faith is not necessarily tied to material wealth or prosperity, as it is primarily spiritual and personal. The Bible often emphasises the importance of faith, such as in **Hebrews 11:1,** which says, "Now faith is the assurance of things hoped for, the conviction of things not seen."

On the other hand, wealth is a subject addressed throughout the Bible as well. While the Bible does not condemn wealth, it warns against the love of money and pursuing wealth as an ultimate goal. In **1 Timothy 6:10**, it is written, "For the love of money is a root of all kinds of evils. It is through this craving that some have wandered away from the faith and pierced themselves with many pangs."

Many Christians believe that being wealthy is not inherently sinful but emphasise that wealth should be used wisely and with a spirit of generosity and stewardship. Wealth should never replace one's faith or become an idol.

The Christian perspective on faith and wealth is that faith should be the cornerstone of one's life, and wealth if obtained, should be managed by one's faith and values, with a focus on helping others and advancing God's kingdom. It is essential for Christians to strike a balance between their pursuit of material wealth and their commitment to spiritual well-being and faithfulness to God.

Faith-Based Investing and Financial Decisions

Faith-based investing and financial decisions are deeply important considerations for Christians who want to align their financial practices with their religious beliefs and values. Understanding stewardship guides financial decisions toward responsible and ethical financial management.

Many faith-based investors seek to avoid investments in companies or industries that contradict their beliefs. This may include companies involved in activities like gambling, alcohol, tobacco, or firearms. It's also important to avoid businesses that support unethical practices, such as labour exploitation or environmental harm.

Faith-based investors often seek opportunities to make a positive impact through their investments. They may prioritise companies that demonstrate responsible corporate practices, support social justice causes, or strongly commit to environmental sustainability.

Some Christians choose to engage in socially Responsible Investing (SRI), which involves investing in companies and funds that align with their values. SRI strategies can vary widely, allowing investors to tailor their portfolios to their specific faith-based priorities.

Christians often turn to the Bible and the teachings of

Jesus for guidance on financial matters. Verses like **Proverbs 3:9-10 encourage** giving to God first, or **Luke 16:10**, which speaks to faithful stewardship, can influence financial decisions.

Many Christians consult financial advisors or investment experts who understand faith-based investing and can help them create a portfolio that aligns with their beliefs while also meeting their financial goals.

Prayer plays a significant role in the financial decision-making process for many Christians. They may seek divine guidance and discernment when making important financial choices.

Faith-based investing and financial decisions involve ensuring that one's money and resources are used in a way that reflects one's faith, values, and commitment to God. While each individual or family may have slightly different priorities and approaches, the underlying principle is to be responsible stewards of the blessings they have received and to make financial decisions that honour one's faith.

Trusting in God's Provision

Trusting in God's provision is a central tenet in Christendom. It involves placing one's faith and confidence in God's ability to provide for our material and spiritual needs in all circumstances. This trust is based on the belief that God is our loving Creator, who knows our needs and cares for us deeply.

The Bible offers several passages that emphasise the importance of trusting in God's provision. One well-known verse is **Matthew 6:25-26**, where Jesus teaches, "Therefore I tell you, do not worry about your life, what you will eat or drink; or about your body, what you will wear. Is not life more than food and the body more than clothes? Look at the birds of the air; they do not sow, reap, or store away in barns, and yet your heavenly Father feeds them. Are you not much more valuable than they?"

This passage encourages us as Christians to cast our anxieties and worries upon God and have faith that He will provide for our daily needs. Trusting in God's provision also involves recognising that while we may work and plan, the ultimate outcome is in God's hands. **Proverbs 16:9** says, "In their hearts, humans plan their course, but the LORD establishes their steps."

Trusting in God's provision does not mean that Christians should become passive or irresponsible in their financial matters. It means acknowledging that all we have ultimately comes from God and that we should manage our resources wisely and with integrity. This includes budgeting, saving, and making prudent financial decisions.

Additionally, trusting in God's provision often involves a spirit of gratitude. We are encouraged to be thankful for what we have and to share our blessings with others, practising generosity and charity as a reflection of God's love.

In challenging times or when facing uncertainty, we should remember God's promise in **Philippians 4:19:** "And my God will meet all your needs according to the riches of his glory in Christ Jesus." This assurance reinforces the idea that, even in difficult circumstances, trusting in God's provision brings peace and hope.

Ultimately, trusting in God's provision is not just about material wealth; it encompasses all aspects of life, including spiritual, emotional, and relational well-being. It reminds believers to rely on God's faithfulness and love in every aspect of their lives.

Balancing Material Wealth with Spiritual Riches

Balancing material wealth with spiritual riches is a fundamental challenge and aspiration for Christians. The Bible offers guidance on finding this equilibrium and understanding the importance of both aspects of life.

Material wealth can bring comfort, security, and the ability to provide for one's family and contribute to the welfare of others. However, it can also lead to greed, materialism, and a misplaced focus on worldly possessions. The Bible warns against the love of money and the pursuit of wealth as the ultimate goal, as mentioned in **1 Timothy 6:10:** "For the love of money is a root of all kinds of evils. It is through this craving that some have wandered away from the faith and pierced themselves with many pangs."

On the other hand, spiritual riches encompass qualities like love, faith, kindness, and a deep relationship with God. These spiritual treasures offer fulfillment, purpose, and eternal significance. Jesus emphasised the value of spiritual riches in Matthew 6:19-21: "Do not store up for yourselves treasures on earth, where moths and vermin destroy, and where thieves break in and steal. But store up for yourselves treasures in heaven, where moths and vermin do not destroy, and where thieves do not break in and steal. For where your treasure is, there your heart will be also."

Finding balance involves recognising that material wealth can enhance one's life and the lives of others when managed responsibly and with a focus on God's purposes. However, it should not become the primary pursuit of one's life. Instead, Christians are encouraged to prioritise spiritual growth, acts of love and kindness, and the pursuit of righteousness.

One way to achieve this balance is through generosity and stewardship. We are taught to be generous with our resources, using our wealth to help those in need and support charitable causes. **Proverbs 19:17** (NIV) illustrates this principle: "Whoever is kind to the poor lends to the LORD, and he will reward them for what they have done."

Regular prayer, Bible study, and participation in Christian communities are also essential for nurturing spiritual riches. These practices help us maintain our focus on God, develop a Christ-like character, and resist the allure of materialism.

The goal is to recognise that spiritual riches are of eternal value, while material wealth is temporary. Balancing the two involves using material wealth to support and enhance one's spiritual journey and the well-being of others rather than allowing it to overshadow the pursuit of spiritual growth and a relationship with God. It's a lifelong journey that requires constant reflection, prayer, and commitment to living by Christian values.

7|| Teaching Generosity and Kingdom Values

As a Christian, we are called to model our lives after the teachings and values of Jesus Christ, who emphasized love, compassion, and generosity throughout His ministry. There are some key principles and approaches to teaching generosity and kingdom values.

The Bible is a rich source of guidance on generosity and Kingdom values. Scriptures like Matthew 6:21 emphasize the importance of aligning one's heart with God's kingdom through generous giving.

Christian leaders, including pastors, parents, and mentors, play a crucial role in teaching generosity. They can model a lifestyle of giving and sacrificial love, showing others how to live out Kingdom values in their daily lives.

Jesus often used parables to convey important Kingdom principles, including generosity. Parables like the Good Samaritan **(Luke 10:25-37)** and the Widow's Offering **(Mark 12:41-44)** can be powerful tools for teaching generosity and compassion.

- Encourage practical acts of generosity, such as giving to the poor, supporting missions, and helping those in need within the community. These activities allow individuals to experience the joy and fulfillment of living out kingdom values.

- Teach the concept of stewardship, emphasizing that all resources, including time, talents, and finances, belong to God. We are called to manage these resources wisely and for the advancement of God's Kingdom.

- Many churches and Christian organizations initiate generosity campaigns and tithing programs to encourage consistent giving. These campaigns often highlight the impact of financial support on ministry and community outreach.

- Host Bible studies, small groups, or Sunday school classes that focus on generosity and Kingdom values. These gatherings can provide opportunities for the in-depth exploration of relevant scriptures and practical applications.

- Share personal testimonies and stories of individuals who have experienced transformation through generosity and Kingdom living. Hearing real-life examples can inspire others to follow suit.

- Encourage prayer for a heart open to God's leading in generosity matters. Praying for God's Guidance and discernment in financial decisions is vital to living out Kingdom values.

- Encourage individuals to regularly evaluate their financial priorities and lifestyles in light of Kingdom values. This reflection can lead to adjustments in spending habits and a deeper commitment to generosity.

Teaching generosity and Kingdom values is not just about financial giving but encompasses a holistic approach to life, guided by love, compassion, and a commitment to God's purposes. It is a lifelong journey of discipleship, where individuals strive to become more Christ-like in their attitudes and actions, thereby contributing to the expansion of God's Kingdom on Earth.

The Biblical Call to Generosity

The Biblical call to generosity is a fundamental theme woven throughout the Old and New Testaments. It's a divine directive that encourages Christians to reflect God's character by giving of themselves, their resources, and their time to benefit others and advance God's Kingdom.

The Bible begins with the story of God's generous creation of the world and humanity. God's giving, starting with the gift of life, sets the foundation for the call to generosity. The pinnacle of this generosity is found in the gift of His Son, Jesus Christ, for the salvation of humanity.

The Old Testament provides numerous examples of generosity, including tithing (giving a tenth of one's income), gleaning laws (leaving part of the harvest for the poor), and offerings to support the Levites and the temple. The story of Abraham's hospitality to strangers **(Genesis 18)** and the generosity of King David are also celebrated.

In the New Testament, Jesus amplifies the call to generosity through His teachings. He emphasizes love for one's neighbour and cares for the marginalized. The parable of the Good Samaritan **(Luke 10:25-37)** explains the importance of selfless giving.

Jesus' life itself is a model of generosity. He healed the sick, fed the hungry, and welcomed sinners. His ultimate act of generosity was His sacrificial death on the cross for the forgiveness of sins. His teaching in **Matthew 25:35-36** shows that acts of kindness and generosity to those in need directly express love for Him.

The early Christian community in **Acts 2:44-45** is described as sharing everything they had with one another, ensuring that no one among them was in need. Their example illustrates the profound impact of generosity within the body of believers.

The Bible encourages cheerful giving, as seen in **2 Corinthians 9:7 (NIV):** "Each of you should give what you have decided in your heart to give, not reluctantly or under compulsion, for God loves a cheerful giver." Generosity is not meant to be a burden but a source of joy and blessing, as explained before.

The Bible also teaches that generosity and giving to the needy are storing treasures in heaven **(Matthew 6:19-21).** It underscores the eternal significance of generosity and how God values it.

Philippians 4:19 assures Christians that God will provide for their needs. Trusting in God's provision can free believers to be more generous.

The biblical call to generosity encourages Christians to give freely, not only of their material resources but also of their time, talents, and love. Through acts of generosity, believers can bring hope, relief, and the message of Christ's love to a hurting world, fulfilling the mandate to be Jesus' hands and feet on Earth.

Fostering a Heart of Compassion in Your Family

- This is a beautiful and essential aspect of living out our Christianity. Compassion, rooted in the love and teachings of Jesus Christ, is the empathy and willingness to help others in their times of need. Here are some ways to cultivate a heart of compassion within the family:

- Model Compassion: As parents or guardians, lead by example. Demonstrate compassion in your daily life, whether it's helping a neighbour, supporting a charitable cause, or showing kindness to strangers. Children often learn best through observation.

- Share Bible Stories: Share Bible stories that highlight compassion and empathy, such as the parable of the Good Samaritan(Luke 10:25-37) or Jesus' healing of the lepers (Luke 17:11-19). Discuss the lessons and values found in these stories together.

- Pray Together: During family prayer times, include prayers for those who are suffering or in need. Praying for others fosters empathy and reminds family members to intercede for those less fortunate.

- Serve as a Family: Engage in volunteer activities or service projects together. This could involve community service, visiting a local shelter, or assisting with church outreach programs. Working together as a family reinforces the value of compassion.
- Discuss Current Events: Use current events as opportunities to discuss compassion and social justice. When news stories highlight suffering or injustice, engage in age-appropriate conversations with your children, helping them understand the importance of compassion in a broken world.
- Encourage Acts of Kindness: Encourage family members to perform random acts of kindness, both within and outside the family. Small gestures of love, like writing notes of encouragement or helping a sibling with a chore, can nurture a compassionate spirit.
- Practice Forgiveness: Teach the importance of forgiveness and reconciliation within the family. This practice promotes compassion and reflects the forgiveness we receive from God through Christ.
- Read Books on Compassion: Explore literature and books that emphasize compassion, empathy, and caring for others. Many children's books and family devotionals are available that focus on these values.
- Discuss Needs vs. Wants: Teach the distinction between needs and wants. Help your family

understand that while it is okay to have desires, prioritizing the needs of others is an important aspect of compassion.

- Express Gratitude: Cultivate gratitude within your family by regularly expressing thanks for what you have. This can help family members appreciate their blessings and become more aware of the needs of others.

- Celebrate Compassion: Acknowledge and celebrate acts of compassion within your family. Recognizing and affirming these behaviours reinforces their importance and encourages further acts of kindness.

- It is an ongoing process that involves intentional teaching, modelling, and practice. By infusing compassion into your family's values and daily life, you not only fulfil a central aspect of Christianity but also contribute to creating a more compassionate and loving world.

Impacting the World through Your Wealth

- As a Christian, the idea of impacting the world through your wealth is deeply rooted in the principles of stewardship, generosity, and a desire to advance God's kingdom on Earth. Here are some ways Christians can consider making a positive impact on the world through financial resources:

- **Prayerful Discernment:** Start by seeking God's guidance and wisdom in how to use your wealth for

His purposes. Regular prayer and seeking His will can help you discern where your resources can significantly impact you.

- **Supporting Missions and Ministries:** Consider financially supporting mission organizations, charities, and ministries that align with your Christian values and are involved in activities such as evangelism, poverty alleviation, education, and healthcare.

- **Humanitarian Aid:** Use your wealth to provide humanitarian aid in times of crisis. This could include responding to natural disasters, providing clean water, food, and medical supplies to those in need, and supporting refugees and displaced populations.

- **Promote Social Justice:** Allocate resources to support causes related to social justice, including advocating for the rights of the marginalized, fighting against human trafficking, and addressing issues of racial equality and poverty.

- **Start or Support Initiatives**: Consider starting or financially supporting initiatives that address specific needs in your community or globally. This could involve establishing a charitable foundation, supporting local schools or healthcare clinics, or funding entrepreneurial ventures with a social impact.

- **Microfinance and Economic Development:** Invest in microfinance programs or small business development initiatives that empower individuals and communities to become self-sustainable. These programs can create jobs and lift people out of poverty.

- **Environmental Stewardship:** Recognize your responsibility to steward God's creation. Use your resources to support environmental conservation efforts and promote sustainable practices that protect the planet.

- **Generosity and Tithing:** Regularly give generously to your church and other Christian organizations. This financial support enables ministries and outreach efforts that positively impact the world.

- **Philanthropic Partnerships:** Collaborate with other individuals, organizations, or foundations to amplify your impact. Combining resources with like-minded individuals or entities can lead to more significant and sustainable change.

- **Lifestyle Choices:** Consider adopting a more modest lifestyle to free up additional resources for charitable giving. Living below your means can allow you to give more generously.

- **Inspire Others:** Share your experiences and testimonies of how God has used your wealth to make an impact. Your story can inspire others to follow suit and contribute to meaningful causes.

- Remember that impacting the world through your wealth is not solely about the amount you give but the heart behind your giving. It's about aligning your financial resources with your Christian values and principles, seeking to be a faithful steward of the blessings God has entrusted to you, and making a positive difference in the lives of others for the glory of God.

8|Navigate Challenges and Trials

The Bible offers guidance, comfort, and hope for Christians facing difficulties. Here are some key principles and perspectives on how to navigate challenges and trials as a Christian:

- **Trust in God's Sovereignty:** Recognize that God is sovereign and controls all circumstances. Even amid trials, trust that God's plan is ultimately for your good and His glory (Romans 8:28).

- **Prayer:** Turn to prayer as a source of comfort and guidance. Share your concerns, fears, and hopes with God in prayer. Philippians 4:6-7 encourages us to "Be anxious for nothing, but in everything by prayer and supplication, with thanksgiving, let your requests be made known to God; and the peace of God, which surpasses all understanding, will guard your hearts and minds through Christ Jesus."

- **Lean on Scripture:** Seek strength and wisdom from the Bible. Many biblical figures faced trials, and their stories can provide inspiration and guidance. Reading verses like Psalm 34:17-18 and Psalm 46:1 can offer comfort in times of trouble.

- **Community and Support:** Surround yourself with a supportive Christian community. Share your burdens with fellow believers who can offer encouragement, prayer, and practical help (Galatians 6:2).

- **Perseverance:** Understand that trials can produce endurance and character growth. James 1:2-4 says, "Consider it pure joy, my brothers and sisters, when everyone faces trials of many kinds because you know that the testing of your faith produces perseverance."

- **Hope in Christ:** Place your hope in Christ and the eternal promises of God. The challenges of this world are temporary, but our hope in Christ is eternal (2 Corinthians 4:17-18).

- **Forgiveness:** Practice forgiveness, both toward others and yourself. Forgiveness is an act of obedience to God and a way to free yourself from the burden of resentment and bitterness (Ephesians 4:31-32).

- **Serve Others:** Sometimes, focusing on helping others in their struggles can provide a sense of purpose and fulfilment. Galatians 5:13 reminds us to "Serve one another in love."

- **Seek Professional Help:** When facing significant challenges such as mental health issues, addiction, or severe trauma, seek professional help. God can work through skilled counsellors and therapists to bring healing and restoration.

- **Patience:** Be patient and wait on God's timing. Sometimes, the resolution to our trials may not come as quickly as we hope, but God's timing is always perfect (Psalm 27:14).

- **Praise and Worship:** Continue to worship and praise God even amid trials. Praising God can shift your focus from the problem to the One who has the power to overcome it (Psalm 34:1).

- **Learn and Grow:** View challenges as opportunities for spiritual growth and learning. God can use trials to refine your faith and draw you closer to Him (1 Peter 1:6-7).

- Navigating challenges and trials as a Christian requires faith, perseverance, and reliance on God's grace. Through prayer, the support of the Christian community, and a steadfast commitment to following Christ, you can find strength and hope even in the midst of life's difficulties.

Facing Financial Difficulties with Faith

Facing financial difficulties with faith is a profound challenge that many Christians encounter at various times. During these times, it's essential to lean on one's faith and rely on God's guidance and provision.

Begin by bringing your financial concerns to God in prayer. Trust that He hears your prayers and cares about your well-being. **Philippians 4:6-7** encourages us: "Do not be anxious about anything but in every situation, by prayer and petition, with thanksgiving, present your requests to God. And the peace of God, which transcends all understanding, will guard your hearts and minds in Christ Jesus."

Ask for God's wisdom in managing your finances, as earlier said. **Proverbs 3:5-6** advises, "Trust in the LORD with all your heart and lean not on your own understanding; in all your ways submit to him, and he will make your paths straight." Consider seeking financial counselling or advice from experienced Christians who can guide you from a biblical perspective.

Cultivate a spirit of contentment and gratitude for what you have, regardless of your financial situation. The Apostle Paul reminds us in Philippians **4:11-12** "I have learned to be content whatever the circumstances. I know what it is to be in need and what it is to have plenty. I have learned the secret of being content in any and every situation, whether well fed or hungry, whether living in plenty or in want."

Create a budget and a financial plan that aligns with your current situation. Stewardship of your resources is a biblical principle, even in difficult times. Proverbs 21:5 states, "The plans of the diligent lead to profit as surely as haste leads to poverty."

Reach out to your Christian community for emotional and practical support. Fellow believers can offer encouragement, prayer, and assistance during challenging financial periods (**Galatians 6:2).**

Consider continuing to tithe and give to your church or other charitable causes, even in tough times. Trust that God will honour your faithfulness. **Malachi 3:10** encourages us: "Bring the whole tithe into the storehouse, that there may be food in my house. Test me in this," says the LORD Almighty, "and see if I will not throw open the floodgates of heaven and pour out so much blessing that there will not be room enough to store it."

Take practical steps to address your financial difficulties, such as reducing unnecessary expenses, exploring additional income sources, and seeking financial advice.

Remember that God is your ultimate provider. He may not always provide in the way you expect or on your timetable but trust that He will meet your needs.

Facing financial difficulties with faith as a Christian requires patience, trust, and reliance on God's promises. It's an opportunity to deepen your faith and witness God's faithfulness in challenging circumstances. Remember that your worth is not determined by your financial situation, and God's love for you remains constant.

Maintaining Family Unity in Times of Adversity

Adversity can come in various forms, such as financial challenges, illness, loss, or relational conflicts. Here are some Christian principles and strategies for preserving family unity during difficult times:

Prayer and Faith: Begin by praying to God as a family. Seek His guidance, strength, and peace during adversity. Encourage family members to exercise faith and trust in God's plan, even when circumstances are tough.

Open Communication: Foster an environment of open and honest communication within the family. Encourage family members to share their feelings, concerns, and fears without judgment. Active listening is crucial during these conversations.

- Bible Study and Devotion: Continue or establish regular family Bible study and devotion times. Reading and discussing scripture can provide comfort, wisdom, and guidance during adversity.

- Support and Encouragement: Be sources of support and encouragement for one another. Galatians 6:2 instructs us to: "Carry each other's burdens, and in this way, you will fulfil the law of Christ." Express love and kindness to family members, offering words of affirmation.

- Gratitude and Perspective: Encourage a perspective of gratitude and counting blessings. Even in adversity, there are often things to be thankful for. Expressing gratitude can shift the family's focus from challenges to blessings.

- Serve Others Together: Find opportunities to serve others as a family, even amid adversity. Acts of service can foster a sense of purpose and unity while helping others in need.

- Respect Differences: Recognize that family members may respond to adversity differently. Some may need space and solitude, while others may seek more support and closeness. Respect each other's coping mechanisms.

- Set Realistic Expectations: Be realistic about what can be achieved during challenging times. Adjust your expectations and prioritize essential tasks.

Avoid overwhelming yourselves with unnecessary stressors.

- Forgiveness and Reconciliation: Emphasize the importance of forgiveness and reconciliation within the family. Adversity can sometimes strain relationships, but forgiveness and reconciliation can bring healing.
- Seek Professional Help: If necessary, consider seeking the assistance of a family counsellor or therapist who can provide guidance and strategies for coping with adversity as a family.
- Lean on Your Faith Community: Your church or faith community can be a valuable source of support during difficult times. Seek fellowship and assistance from fellow believers who share your faith and values.
- Maintain Hope: Encourage a sense of hope within the family. Remind each other of God's promises and the assurance that He is with you through every trial (Isaiah 41:10).
- Maintaining family unity in times of adversity is a testament to the strength of faith and the power of love within a Christian family. By drawing on your faith, practising patience, and supporting one another, you can navigate adversity together, emerging stronger and more united as a family.

Trusting God's Plan for Your Family's Future

It involves surrendering your desires and ambitions to God's sovereign will and placing your faith in His wisdom, guidance, and provision.

Begin by seeking God's will through prayer. Engage in earnest, heartfelt prayer as a family, asking God to guide your decisions and reveal His plan for your family's future. Jesus' example of praying, "Your will be done" (Matthew 6:10), is a powerful reminder of our dependence on God's guidance.

We should regularly study and meditate on God's Word as a family. Scripture provides wisdom, comfort, and direction for every aspect of life, including family decisions. **Psalm 119:105** tells us, "Your word is a lamp for my feet, a light on my path."

Trust that God controls your family's future, even when circumstances seem uncertain. **Proverbs 19:21** reminds us, "Many are the plans in a person's heart, but the LORD's purpose prevails."

Embrace the principle of submission and surrender to God's will. This means being willing to let go of your own plans and desires if they do not align with God's purpose for your family.

Cultivate an attitude of contentment and gratitude for where your family is presently. Gratitude fosters an appreciation for God's blessings and helps you trust His provision for the future.

Seek counsel from mature and spiritually grounded Christians, such as pastors or trusted friends, when making significant family decisions. **Proverbs 15:22** advises, "Plans fail for lack of counsel, but with many advisers, they succeed."

Be open to God's redirection and guidance, even if it leads your family on a different path than you initially envisioned. God's plan will unfold differently from our own, and flexibility is essential.

Understand that God's timing may not align with your own. Be patient and persevere through trials and waiting periods, trusting God is working for your family's good **(Romans 8:28).**

Place your faith in God's character and His promises. Trust that He is faithful, loving, and all-knowing. Hebrews 11:6 reminds us that "without faith, it is impossible to please God because anyone who comes to him must believe that he exists and that he rewards those who earnestly seek him."

Remember that, as Christians, our ultimate hope is not solely in this earthly life but in the eternal life promised through Jesus Christ. Your family's future is ultimately secure in Him.

Trusting God's plan for your family's future can be challenging, especially when uncertain or difficult. However, a journey of faith allows you to experience God's guidance, peace, and purpose in every season of life. As you surrender your family's future to Him, you can rest assured that He is the faithful author of your story, leading you toward a future filled with His blessings and grace.

Conclusion

The foundations of faith and family are essential pillars of the Christian life, extending to the concept of generational wealth. As Christians, we are called to build a legacy of faith, values, and financial stewardship that transcends generations. A biblical guide to generational wealth is not merely about accumulating material riches but about passing on the spiritual and moral principles that align with God's Word.

From a biblical perspective, generational wealth is built on trust in God's provision, diligent stewardship, and a commitment to living out Kingdom values. It involves teaching the next generation to honour God with their resources, be generous to those in need, and use their wealth to advance God's kingdom on Earth.

Foundations of faith and family are intertwined with the pursuit of generational wealth, reminding us that our earthly resources are temporary. Still, the impact of our faith and values can leave an indelible mark on our descendants. This journey requires prayer, guidance from God's Word, and a heart committed to living out Christ's teachings.

As we strive to build generational wealth with faith and family at its core, let us remember the words of **Joshua 24:15**: "But as for me and my household, we will serve the LORD." Let's ensure our families are known not only for their financial success but also for their unwavering faith, integrity, and commitment to following Christ, leaving a legacy that honours God for generations to come.